The Construction of
the Mother Church

Reminiscences

of

Edward P. Bates, C.S.D.

Healing Unlimited is pleased to present this volume in the interest of preserving a sacred and important history concerning the development and efficacy of Christian Science and a fuller understanding of the life and teachings of Mary Baker Eddy, the Discoverer, Founder and Leader of Christian Science. Other titles (abbreviated) include those in *The Carpenter Collection of Works on Christian Science* offered by the publisher:

500 Watching Points   Items by and about MBE Culled from the Press
Reminiscences of Henrietta Chanfrau   *Collectanea*
Destiny of the Mother Church   *Memoirs of Mary Baker Eddy*
Divinity Course   *Early Verse of Mary Baker Eddy*
Essays ascribed to Mary Baker Eddy   *Footprints Fadeless*
Fragments   Recollections of Mary Baker Eddy, by James Gilman
Instruction in Metaphysics   *Address on Christian Science*
Man and Woman   Mary Baker Eddy: Her Spiritual Footsteps
Mary Baker Eddy: Her Spiritual Precepts, Miscellaneous Documents
Notes on Metaphysical Obstetrics   Notes on Metaphysical Work
Poems   Private Directions for Metaphysical Healing
Prospectus of The Carpenter Foundation   Questions and Answers
Watches, Prayers, Arguments   Visions of Mary Baker Eddy
Mary Baker Eddy as I Knew Her   Ira O. Knapp and Flavia Knapp
The Genealogy of Asa G. Eddy

The electronic (digital) searchable version of this book is available from the publisher.

Above titles will be available during 2010 and 2011 from the publisher, Healing Unlimited:

800.962.1464 • www.ChristianScience.org • heal@christianscience.org

ISBN: 978-1-893107-14-4

The Construction of the Mother Church

Reminiscences of
Edward P. Bates, C.S.D.

Introduction

In January, 1887, Edward and Caroline Bates took Primary Class with Mrs. Eddy. They took Normal Class under Mrs. Eddy in October, 1887, and a second Normal Class with her in March, 1889. This was Mrs. Eddy's last class taught in the Metaphysical College. In 1887, Mr. Bates was asked to preach in The Mother Church on alternate Sundays, before the Lesson Sermon was instituted. Also in this year, he and his wife taught Christian Science classes in Syracuse, New York, and New Haven, Connecticut, among other places. In 1892, they were appointed First Members of The First Church of Christ, Scientist, in Boston.

At the World's Fair in Chicago in 1893, Mr. Bates gave one of the addresses, at the request of Mrs. Eddy.

Mr. Bates was instrumental in obtaining

permission to purchase from the Oxford University Press in England, the thin, strong paper heretofore used only for Bibles. At first they refused his request, but when it was shown that the sale of Science and Health increased the sale of Bibles, they agreed to sell the paper to the Publishing Society. (William Dana Orcutt, Mary Baker Eddy and Her Books, pp.60-68)

From November, 1894 to its completion and dedication, Mr. Bates at Mrs. Eddy's request, supervised the construction of The Mother Church as the Board's assistant. He was President of The Mother Church for four terms, a member of the Board of Directors, and a Trustee of the Christian Science Publishing Society. In addition to the tremendous time and effort given by the Bateses, Mrs. Bates donated a rose window to The Mother Church. She also designed the sunburst skylight in the auditorium.

Mrs. Eddy refers to Mr. and Mrs. Bates in her Dedicatory Sermon for The Mother Church. (*Pulpit and Press*, page 9) Other references to Mr. and Mrs. Bates are in *Pulpit and Press*: 59:25; 77:20; 78:18; 171:26; *Miscellany*: pages 319-322. (An important letter by Mr. Bates.)

Joseph Armstrong, in Building of The Mother Church, refers to Mr. Bates' work in supervising construction of the building.

Mrs. Eddy wrote about Mr. Bates as "the most

helpitive student I ever had." (*Longyear Quarterly News*, Vol. 23, No. 2, Summer, 1986)

These reminiscences are a wonderful accounting of what love for our Leader can accomplish and the obedience it instills. The moral courage and obedience of Mr. and Mrs. Bates enabled our Leader to build her church. It is the same moral courage and obedience that will keep it with us.

The Mother Church

It was during the year 1893 that plans were made to build The Mother Church edifice at the intersection of Norway and Falmouth Streets, on a piece of property owned by Mrs. Eddy which she had bought with the intention of having erected thereon a church edifice.

After the close of the exhibition, Mrs. Eddy invited me to her home in Concord, New Hampshire. She desired to consult with me about the material to be used in building the exterior of the church. She said, "We have talked about brick, but I should like Concord granite."

"You can have it," I replied.

She said, "It will cost a great deal of money—a great many thousand dollars more than it would to build it of brick."

I replied that there was plenty of money, and

only one source of supply.

She said, "Do you believe it?"

I answered, "Yes."

She said, "Wait a minute." Going up-stairs, she wrote a letter to the Directors of the church in which she authorized them to build the exterior of the church of Concord granite. She asked me to take it to Boston and deliver it, which I did.

The foundation was then being prepared and brought up nearly to the grade line and afterwards covered up for the winter. In the spring the building operations were resumed. The contract was given to a reliable firm, and the granite was duly sent to Boston so that it could be used in the construction of the exterior.

In July, I prepared the plans for the heating and ventilation of the church at the request of the Board of Directors. The building operations proceeded slowly. In October, 1894, Mrs. Bates and I went to Boston where I attended a meeting of the Publishing Committee. In company with two ladies from New York, we visited the church edifice and were somewhat surprised at its incompleteness. We decided to take an early train to Concord the next morning and call on Mrs. Eddy to consult with her about what could be done to accelerate the building of the church. We went to Concord and called at the house, told the object of our coming, and our desire to consult with Mrs. Eddy. After waiting some time, a student brought a message from Mrs. Eddy which was to the effect that we should return to Boston and do our work. We were greatly disappointed at not seeing her, but we could do no other than obey. We returned to our hotel in Boston and remained there three or four days, working to the best of our ability, and then returned to Syracuse.

It was during this interval that an error was revealed which I had not anticipated. In conversation with the Directors, we found that they had stopped making contracts for finishing the church as there was very little or no money in the treasury,—barely enough to pay for the contracts which were in force. Everything seemed dead. The Publishing Committee went into executive session and gave this matter serious consideration. Finally, it was unanimously voted to give the Directors ten thousand dollars, which we had in the bank, towards the completion of the church.

The following day there was a First Members' meeting and we reported this decision. It did not seem to be received in the spirit which I had anticipated. We called upon the treasurer of the church to report the amount of money in the treasury and found there was between four and five thousand dollars. Then we called upon the treasurer of the building fund and he made his report. I then made a motion that the treasurer of the church should pay over to the treasurer of the building fund four thousand dollars. This raised a storm, and before I knew it, we had two churches,—an old church and a new church,—with no connection between them. I argued the thing to the best of my ability, as did several of the other members, but to no avail. The treasurer said if everybody else voted for it, she would not pay over the money.

If I remember correctly, the National Association had funds, and the treasurer of that Association was asked to turn over the money to the treasurer of the building fund. This did not seem to meet with favor. I tried to impress upon the members the necessity of immediately transferring the money so that the work of the church could go on, but my plea did not meet with a favorable response from all the members, although many of them were in favor of it.

That night one of the members reported to Mrs. Eddy what had been done, and she sent down a letter of approval to the Publishing Committee for their decision and authorized the church treasurer to turn over the money to the treasurer of the building fund. This, however, was never done as will be shown later. Abraham thought he had a call to offer up Isaac, his only son, and when he was ready to make the offering, his hand was stayed.

In this meeting of the First Members, I asked permission to write Edward A. Kimball of Chicago and some of the large churches in New York and other cities to increase their subscriptions to the building fund. This permission was granted. It was immediately taken up. The Journal was also authorized to publish a card of the same purport. This, of course, reached the entire field. The consequence was that money came in by the thousands and tens of thousands, and Mr. Chase was kept busy late at night signing receipts for the money. Mr. Kimball did a wonderful work for us in Chicago and through the West, and Chicago met the case grandly and sent on check after check of large amounts until we had money in abundance.

It will be remembered that in December Mr. Chase was obliged to send a notice through the next Journal to stop sending money as we had enough and too much, and that no money would be received which was sent after a certain date. I know of no parallel to this except where Moses built the Tabernacle in the Wilderness: "And they spake unto Moses, saying, The people bring much more than enough for the service of the work which the Lord commanded to make. And Moses gave commandment, and they caused it to be proclaimed throughout the camp, saying, Let neither man nor woman make any more work for the offering of the sanctuary. So the people were restrained from bringing. For the stuff they had was sufficient for all the work to make it, and too much." (Exodus 36:5-7) Surely the church was being resurrected.

On the fifth of November, we went to Boston to attend the monthly meeting of the Christian Science Publishing Society. A friend of ours, a young architect living in the East, had been to Chicago on business, and was about to return home. I asked him if he would accompany us to Boston as I wanted him to see the designs of the windows in the church, particularly the rose window in the north wall which Mrs. Bates presented to the church, the subject being the raising of Jairus' daughter. Mrs. Eddy suggested the subject, which had been used as a frontispiece in one of the early editions of Science and Health. While we were representing the Publishing Society in Chicago the year before, he came there and we spent a great deal of time examining the cathedral glass designs of Tiffany and of various other manufacturers. I saw that he was familiar with this class of work and had given it much study. I, myself, had given it some study, as I had been in Europe in 1891 and had visited many of the fine cathedrals and made a specialty of studying the windows as well as the mosaic work. Finding that he was conversant with art glass in its various phases, I said to Mrs. Bates, "He will be a good man to help us on the window next year," to which she assented. Nothing was said about it then, but in November we asked him to go and criticise the window, its design, color and effect in general.

This he consented to do.

We arrived in Boston on the fifth of November, as stated. During the day, we went to the studio of the firm who had the contract for the windows, and there met the Directors and two or three members of the church who were especially interested in the windows and the decorations. Mrs. Bates' gift was examined critically and passed on, some suggestions being made which were accepted. The opposite rose window given by the Directors was also examined and found to be a very beautiful window and typical of various symbols and signs, which are described in a book by Mr. Armstrong entitled *The Mother Church*.

While there the architect cast his eye over the plans in general and observed something which I had not seen because I had taken for granted that the plans were right, and it was not my place to criticise them, in any event; he found that the ceiling trusses of the auditorium were three feet too low where they rested on the wall between the gallery and the vestibule. In fact, they were so low that a person would have to stoop to get into the gallery, and then the rear seats of the gallery could not be made available. I was shocked at this and immediately called the attention of the Board of Directors to the defect. They were surprised, and asked what we should do. I said, "There is but one thing to do, and that is to raise the trusses. The wall is there, heavy enough to carry it, and if we raise the trusses three feet you can enter the gallery and the rear seats will be available for use."

They said, "Yes, but the contract is let for the ceiling trusses; they are being gotten out, and there is no time to lose." There were many other questions that came up, and finally we saw that the Board of Directors were inclined to employ this architect to finish the church. One of them said, "God has sent this man here and we need him."

Arrangements were made the following day for him to take up the work of the interior and carry it to a conclusion. He remained with us in Boston four days. We were discussing how we could change the curve of the ceiling trusses.

On Wednesday afternoon, the seventh, I met with the Directors and the matter was thoroughly canvassed. My opinion was that if the ceiling, near the wall on which the trusses rested, could not be raised the church should not be completed, and they agreed with me; the question was, could it be done?

I said, "Certainly it could."

Could it be done without delaying the finishing of the church?

"Yes."

Each Director had in his pocket a letter from

Mrs. Eddy demanding that the church be ready for service in 1894. The completion of the edifice seemed a long way off,—much longer than that time. Finally Mr. Chase, the treasurer, said, "Mr. Bates, will you agree to look after the raising of that ceiling and not delay the finishing of the church?"

I immediately said, "Yes," and then I felt I had committed an almost unpardonable sin for I had no right to promise anything. All of the arguments which could be presented were presented mentally, and I was ready to withdraw from the contract.

Mr. Chase said, "What do you want?" I said, "I want a letter from the Directors to the president of the Boston Bridge Company."

"What shall I say?"

I said, "Authorize him to turn his whole shop over to me; his draftsmen, engineers, superintendent and workmen, and I will remedy the defect." He wrote the letter I asked for and signed it.

It was then between five and six o-clock. I called up the office of the Boston Bridge Company and asked for the president. He was absent and would not be in again that evening. I found he lived in Auburndale, and took the first train there. I went to his house, and was very graciously met by his wife. She informed me that her husband would probably not be home until eight or nine o'clock. I said, "With your permission I will wait."

She said, "He is going to New York at eleven o'clock and will be gone several days."

I then saw the need of prompt action. I waited for him and about nine o'clock he came in. He read the letter from the Board of Directors. "Well, Mr. Bates, that is rather a broad request;—what do you want?"

"I want just what that letter calls for. I want your works,—your superintendent, your engineers, your draftsmen and your workmen, until I get through with them."

"Very well," he said, and wrote a letter to his superintendent. I thanked him very much. He went to New York and I went to Boston.

Early the next morning the architect and myself went to Cambridge to the office of the Boston Bridge Company, and were there when the doors were opened. We had met two of the engineers and found them very congenial people. We asked them to bring in the superintendent and foreman of the shop, which they did. We stated the object of our visit. The plans were on the drafting board and the changes necessary in order to make the auditorium a proper place in which to hold service were clearly apparent. After studying it a long time the chief engineer said, "Mr. Bates, it will take eight weeks to change the plans."

I said, "Impossible." I saw what he meant, and recognized that he had good reason for his statement; but I told him that in eight weeks we must have service in that church. We talked there as long as it was profitable. I found all the men in the Company gentlemanly and courteous, and willing to do everything that could be done, but none of them could do impossibilities.

I finally suggested that we go to the church and make a survey of the conditions. They consented, and we went to the church together and went up in the gallery. What a scene it was! Bare beams covered with ice and snow; slippery planks with a steep pitch where anything could slide off into the auditorium; it was a most forbidding day and conditions. We managed in some way to get a footing and examined the walls to see what could be done. We remained there a long time examining the building and conferring about the method of making changes. Finally the chief engineer said, "Mr. Bates, we can do it." and he told me how.

I said, "Yes, you will do it."

In eight days new ceiling trusses were in place, ready for the lighter beams and lathing. I was relieved of my promise to the Directors.

We must not overlook the fact that Mrs. Eddy was at her home in Concord demonstrating for the church.

This was on Thursday, the eighth of November. So far as I am informed, the fall had been the worst that Boston ever knew. It was worse than the winter when the Pilgrims landed. Snow came in October and remained. The roof was not on the church, which was filled with snow and ice for several inches, and was a terrible place to work in. A few workmen were about the church proceeding in a nonchalant way, and little was accomplished to advance the building. Several superintendents had been employed by the Directors, who, no doubt, were competent men; but they all quit from time to time, and at that time no one was in charge of the work except the various contractors, and they were accomplishing little. This brought to my mind a long train of thought. I felt I had a duty to do.

That night I took the train for Albany and transferred to a train for Plattsburg, New York, where I had an important business appointment on Friday. I slept very little that night; a conflict was going on between my sense of duty to the church and my desire to mind my own business and let the church alone. I realized what would happen if I gave up my time to the church, and to me the outlook was far from pleasant. If I went to Syracuse and minded my own business, I would get along all right. So argument followed argument until finally I decided that I would offer my services to the Board of Directors.

I went to Plattsburg on Friday and returned to Syracuse that night. On Saturday I wired the Directors asking them to meet me at Publishing rooms on Monday morning as I had an important matter to communicate to them. In the afternoon of that day the architect wired me that he had been discharged. I wired back, telling him to keep at work until I discharged him. He kept at work.

Monday morning, we met in the Publishing rooms,—all the Directors present. I said, "Gentlemen, I have come to Boston to offer you my services. You need someone constantly at the church to take care of this work and see that it progresses rapidly. I feel that I can do this, and if you wish to accept of my services I will give you my time until it is finished." They immediately accepted and wrote a letter authorizing me to take charge of the structure, to make contracts, and to do everything which the Board of Directors was authorized to do. I said, "Gentlemen, you will find me at the church in the future."

This was the twelfth of November. Seven weeks remained until the day Mrs. Eddy had designated for the opening service. The roof was not on, no windows were in, the building was full of snow and ice. Very little was being done to advance the progress of the building.

Mrs. Bates found a suite of rooms at the Hotel Santa Monica on Huntington Avenue, nearly opposite the end of Norway Street. The location was convenient. Nine rooms on the top floor gave us plenty of space for the drafting room, sleeping room for the architect and ourselves, and room for our friends who were coming from New York to work for the church.

I went into the church and found but a few men there and none of the contractors. I sent for the contractors, and as they came someone usually told them that I did not want to see them and that their class of work would not be wanted for two or four or six weeks; that they would be sent for when their work was wanted. This sort of thing continued for several days. I finally became acquainted with the contractors, knew their names and faces and got them organized, and was proceeding with the work.

The hotel was so near that it seemed agreeable to me to go there to lunch, although I never cared much about lunch after I was healed. The first day I went to lunch because it would be a social matter with Mrs. Bates. When I came back into the church, everything was disorganized. It took me all the afternoon to recover my position. The second day I again went to lunch at noon and the results were similar to the first day. This convinced me that I had a duty to perform and, ever after until the church was finished, I remained there from eight in the morning until five at night, or later, if we worked overtime. I cared nothing for the lunch except the sociability of it, but I did care for the thought which was forced on the workmen. After a few days I succeeded in forming a good organization and increasing the number of workmen until we had twenty contractors and over two hundred men hard at work for the desired end. We took up work which the contractors said the building was not ready for, while I insisted that it was.

Mosaic Work

Wood floors and wood wainscoting had been planned for the church. During our trip to Europe three years before, we had become very much interested in mosaic work of many grades and styles. We had seen one big church at Monreale, near Palermo, which was entirely lined with mosaics from the floor to the apex of the roof. This work was very elaborate, very beautiful in color and design. The lower part illustrated, according to the conception of the artist, the creation of the world in heroic figures. The upper part of the walls was covered with mosaics illustrating the twelve Apostles. The beauty of the work from the mechanical and artistic standpoint was very attractive. The church also had massive bronze doors—among the most beautiful we had ever seen. Many other public buildings and cathedrals through Europe were visited which had mosaic work.

After returning from Europe, we constantly referred to the beauty of the mosaic work which we had seen, and when it was decided to erect our church, we hoped that mosaic work might be used in it. During our visit to Boston in October, we had consulted with the Directors; and after the money began to come in, they were convinced that the floors and dado should be of this material and the contract was let. This has always been very satisfactory.

I remember very well my conversation with the firm who had the contract for the mosaic work. Very soon after I was put in charge of the work, I sent for them and told them I was ready to have the mosaic floor laid in the auditorium. They looked at me as though I had escaped from some institution for the feebleminded. I said, "I mean it."

"Why, Mr. Bates," one said, "it is impossible."

"Well," said I, "I can't help that,—we have got to have it."

He said, "Nobody but a fool would think of it."

I said, "I agree with you. Several wise men were here on this building. They did not make any progress on it,—so they got a fool down here from the country who proposed to do something. The reason I am here is because I don't know much about building. I don't know much about the conventional rules of builders, and don't propose to follow them. I came here to get this building finished and we shall have to set aside all building rules to get the building so we can occupy it."

He refused to do anything on his contract. He said, "The roof isn't on. It will spoil the work."

I said, "I will take care of the roof, and I will take care of your work when you get it in, but the mosaics I must have."

After several hours' argument, he conceded the point, saying, "If this work is spoiled it will be your fault."

I said, "I will take the blame for it, but I must have it done."

He said, "I never heard of putting a mosaic floor in a building without a roof," and I said, "No, I haven't either, but we are going to do it here." Part of the roof was on and I felt that we could protect his work in some way until the remainder was finished. He soon began operations, had a fine lot of workmen, and the work progressed well. He laid a good floor, and we covered it up with sawdust and boards.

We were then ready to build a scaffold to plaster

the ceiling and side walls. The laying of the mosaic was the key to the situation, as will be seen later.

At about this time one of the workmen came to me,—a brick layer, a very intelligent man, and said, "Mr. Bates, you are the queerest man I ever saw. You have been around here several weeks and I have never seen you looking at a plan."

I said, "I don't need to. I read the plans when I first came and I don't need to consult them. What I am doing is to get the building finished." He thought it strange.

I soon began to encourage the contractor for plastering to build his scaffold. He said it was useless, but I led him gently along as well as I could; he finally commenced, with reluctance, and the scaffolding grew. The lighter rafters between the trusses were being laid and it would soon be time to lath the ceiling, and I wished him to be ready as every moment was valuable. He made progress, and the scaffold was finally completed so that the lathers could work on it.

About this time it became necessary to look after the sidewalk outside the church. The weather was bitter cold. Concrete would freeze in two or three hours. E. Noyes Whitcomb, who had the contract for finishing the interior of the church, was my faithful ally. He was a noble man, a courteous gentleman, who afterwards became a Scientist and joined the church. We had talked over the matter of the sidewalk, and I asked him to go to Atlantic Avenue to some sail loft and get a sufficient number of old sails to go entirely around the church. He saw the point in a moment and got the sails. We fastened them to the wall of the church above the basement windows and carried them out on an angle to the roadway outside the curb. The heat was in the church, and we had put cotton cloth in the windows to retain it, and the building was being warmed very comfortably. We took the windows out of the basement and for two or three days let the heat out over the sidewalk. It drew the frost out of the ground and then we began the walk, which we built without cessation; it proved to be a good structure. The canvas was kept in place until the walk was thoroughly dry and there was no danger of deterioration from frost, when it was removed.

While the church was in progress of construction, Mr. Whitcomb came in one morning with a very melancholy cast of countenance. I asked him what was the matter with him and he told me what he thought, which was serious enough, if it could not be removed. I said to him, "Why don't you take some of my medicine?" He said he had tried it to some extent. Said I, "Have you studied the book?" He replied that he had not. "Well," I said, "that is the medicine. Didn't the party who treated you advise you to study the book?"

He said, "No."

I replied to him, "Mr. Whitcomb, I think you are mistaken. The party who treated you must have asked you to read the book; you may have overlooked it. You did not think it of enough consequence. Now I will make a prescription for you. Go to the city, buy a book and read it."

He answered, "I have no time."

"How is your time occupied?"

"Well," he said, "for ten hours I am about my contracts, and at home I have to make estimates and write and do various things, which consume my entire evening."

I then told him if he didn't take time to read the book, he wouldn't have time to do anything very long. He admitted it. He finally agreed to buy a book and study it. I recommended him to go to one of the older students who would do good work and have treatment for a few days, to take his medicine every night and accept it whether the statements antagonized him or not, and he would be healed. After a few weeks, he came to me, his face beaming with joy. He said, "Mr. Bates, I am a well man. I did what you told me to do, and I am perfectly well for the first time in several years." Other contractors and workmen were healed during the progress of the work of the church.

Plastering the Church

On Friday, the eighth of December, Mrs. Bates received a short but emphatic letter from Mrs. Eddy. It read, "Finish the Tower and plaster the Church." This letter produced a great deal of turbulence in my mind and some outward expression of it.

I asked, "Why did Mrs. Eddy send this letter to Mrs. Bates? Why did she not send it to the Directors or to me?" The messenger replied that the letter was for Mrs. Bates. I asked many other questions. Then I looked about the church. It was not ready to plaster. How could Mrs. Eddy, up in Concord, know that we should plaster the church? We were on the ground pushing the work along as rapidly as possible; in fact, more rapidly than the contractors thought possible. To have this peremptory order seemed very singular to us. It was a command. And whether we would recognize it or not, Mrs. Eddy had a good reason for making it.

We talked it over through the day and went to our rooms and talked about it all night. I recognized the fact that the church should be plastered, but how to get it done was the point at issue. The lathing of the ceiling of the auditorium was not finished. I had succeeded in getting the scaffolding in place and a series of electric lights arranged so that the workers could see on the scaffold, and was advancing the work generally as rapidly as I knew how, but I could not see how we could plaster it immediately. One point in the discussion was the resistance of the plaster contractor. I knew what he would say as well as I knew it when I made the proposal to him. I knew all his arguments, and knew what I should say and do in rebuttal.

When morning came, I went to the church at eight o'clock and looked for the contractor. He had been doing some desultory work under the galleries; I had encouraged him in this so that he would have some men on the job and be interested in it. About nine o'clock he came in. The day was one of the worst I ever saw in Boston or any other place. It had been snowing for several weeks, occasionally freezing and thawing and raining until, on Huntington Avenue, to illustrate, there was nearly a foot of snow and ice hard frozen and full of ruts and chuck holes. A gale was blowing from the northeast and rain came in torrents. It was a most forbidding day, one in which no man should go on the street.

When the contractor came into the church, I said to him, "I want to have a little talk with you."

"Go ahead," he said.

"There is so much noise in this auditorium we can hardly be heard; let us step out here at the Norway Street exit and I will talk with you."

"It is cold out there," he said.

"I know that."

He said, "You will take a cold,—you have no overcoat."

I said, "I will not take cold."

We went out there and I proposed to him that we begin plastering the church auditorium that night. He turned on his heel and started to go back. I happened to be nearest to the door and said, "Hold on a minute, we must talk this thing over."

He told me that the ceiling was not lathed; they could not do it.

"The ceiling can be lathed," I said.

He said, "It will not be lathed in time to put on any plaster to-night."

I told him I thought it would. We talked along this line perhaps half an hour and then he told me I should go inside,—I would freeze out there. It was cold enough in the air, but I was warm enough within to take care of me,—in fact, I had all the heat that a man could stand without exploding, which would not do under the present conditions.

He then came out flatly and said, "Mr. Bates, I

have heard much talk about having a service in this church this year. You may as well know now what is going to be done here. I will be plastering in this church ten or twelve weeks from to-day. There will be no service held here because the building cannot be finished."

I replied, "Never mind that part of it. What I want is to get the auditorium plastered; we will take care of the other part when it comes."

He said, "Nonsense,—there is no use to talk about it—I am going in,—I am freezing out here."

"Wait a minute," I said, "we will talk a little further." And so, without repeating the conversation, we stayed there over two hours. At the end of that time he agreed to get the plaster, send a man to the exchange and order up the men to put it on with the necessary help. It was then about eleven-thirty. The minutes that morning were worth years to me, and I could hardly wait to get at a culmination of the matter. I said, "Let us go to the telephone and order the plaster." We needed twenty-four tons.

He said, "I am going right to my office and I will order it."

I said, "Let us go up here on Massachusetts Avenue and order it now and save time; it will make a difference perhaps at the warehouse."

He said, "No, I am going right to my office. I will

be there in ten minutes, and I will order it."

"You will remember that we need twenty-four tons?"

"Oh, yes," he said, "I will order it." I have reason to believe he did not.

He sent a man to the exchange and ordered the plasterers and tenders. That was correctly done. I advised him to tell them that every man who went on the scaffold would receive a bonus of ten dollars.

My mistake was not going to the telephone with him as is my custom at such a critical time. I believe in finishing what I undertake. But he was so positive he would do this work that I could hardly, with good manners, insist on anything else.

I waited with some apprehension until two o'clock or after, telling the man who tended the lower door to let me know when the plaster arrived. He came up and said, "Mr. Bates, there is a load of plaster here."

"Send in the teamster,—I want to see him." He came.

"How much have you on?" I asked.

"Four tons."

"Where is the rest of your load?"

He replied, "There were six or eight teams of us at the warehouse under a shed all the morning with seven tons of plaster on each gondola, and we had an order to take it up to an apartment house on Beacon Street. We waited until noon and unloaded it because they telephoned from the apartment that the building was loaded with plaster already delivered and they could not take care of any more. So all the teams but mine drove in, unloaded, and went home. I took off three tons and came up here."

Said I, "How is that?"

"Why," he said, "only four were ordered."

This was a shock to me. "Well," I said, "you will go back and get another load, won't you?"

"No," he said, "I wouldn't go back on such a day as this for any living man; I am going to the stable to unhitch." I reasoned with him but he was firm in his refusal to bring up another load of plaster. I was obliged to let him go.

A friend of mine on Massachusetts Avenue had a telephone and offered me the use of it freely; I made free use of it that afternoon telephoning. First I tried the warehouse; the only response was, "Call again, the line is busy,—call again, the line is busy." This continued, probably, for over half an hour. I finally succeeded in getting the warehouse and inquired, "Where are the other twenty tons of plaster?"

He said, "You have all that you ordered."

"Well," I said, "we intended to order twenty-four tons."

"I don't care anything about that," he retorted, "I got the order for four tons and sent it up. I am going to lock up and go home. This is not a fit day for a man to be out, and what's more, the teams have all been put up and the men have gone home."

"My dear friend," I replied, "you must not lock up your warehouse until I get twenty tons of plaster out of it."

He said, "Who are you? I never knew you nor saw you."

"My name is Bates," I replied, "but I represent the Board of Directors of the Christian Science Church."

"Well," he said, "I don't know anything about that."

"I will tell you another thing," was my answer. "The specification was made for a different class of plaster and I had it changed because I considered yours a better grade,—now you owe me some consideration for that. What is more, your manager is from Syracuse and is one of my personal friends; he would do anything to forward this matter if he knew about it."

"He is not here," he replied. "He has gone away. We always close Saturday afternoons."

"Whatever comes," I said, "you must keep the warehouse open until I get the plaster."

"I will not do anything of the kind," he replied.

I said, "If I don't get gondolas to take it up, I will get hacks and express wagons, but I must have it to-night."

He said, "You don't get it out of this place." After further conversation, he consented to keep the warehouse open for a short time to see if we could get teams.

I said, "You are here in the business, you know the people that have teams. You can get hold of them."

"Yes," he said, "I had them here. We had more plaster loaded than you could use up there, but I had to unload it and let the teams go home." He then gave me the names of some carting firms, and I called them up with a result that was not agreeable.

I first called one and I got the word back, "Call again, the line is busy." And so I worked for a long time. Finally I got one trucking firm. I said, "Will you send your teams down to Atlantic Avenue to get us some plaster for the church?"

Said he, "No sir, my teams are in and they are in till Monday morning. I wouldn't send a team out on a day like this for any man. We don't know you and we can't send the teams."

I reasoned and argued with him, showing him my plight. It was of no avail. I then called up another trucking firm. After being refused the use of the line a long time, I succeeded in getting them and asked them to send for this plaster. I got a flat refusal. Their teams were in where they ought to be on such a day. It was not a fit day to have a team out in the street, and they would not take up a load for any money I chose to offer. I called a third trucking firm and the same reply was given. It was then about four-thirty. I had been at the telephone over two hours and all I had succeeded in doing was to keep the plaster warehouse open. My friend the manager lived on Westland Avenue, and I concluded it was about time for his return.

A Scientist came to the office and I asked him to take the telephone and see what he could do while I went to see my friend. I found him just arrived and I told him my story. He said, "Mr. Bates, you shall have the plaster."

Said I, "Can I go to the church and be sure that

you will deliver that plaster,—some of it immediately and all of it by midnight?"

He said, "Yes sir, we will do it." So I went back to the church, arriving there probably about four forty-five.

It was a dark day, the clouds hung low; I couldn't see any light inside the building. I went into the lower vestibule and groped my way to the stairs and to the upper vestibule. I found the church in darkness. There were two kerosene torches and two or three hand lanterns, and no other light. I asked what happened to the electric current. I was told the storm had broken the wires an hour or two before and there was no electricity in the building,—there was none in that part of the city.

The plastering contractor came to me, a good deal hotter than I was in the morning, but with a more decided tendency to tell what he felt, and he opened quite a tirade on me, blaming me for all these conditions. I did not ask him why he ordered only four tons of plaster instead of twenty-four, and never did, because it would do no good. It would not have changed matters, and he would probably have left the church in disgust. He said, "I have all this force of men to put this plaster on, and all we have in the church is four tons."

"We will have more soon," I replied.

"Where are we going to get it?" he asked.

"It is coming," I said.

"Where are the lights?" was his next retort. "My men can't work without lights."

I said, "The lights will be on." But he kept on sputtering and ventilating himself until nearly five o'clock.

The men remained, and at five o'clock the electric lights broke out. I said, "Boys, to the scaffold!" and away they went. We had put up two very strong ladders, one for the ascending column, and one for the descending, and we started the mortar upward and the empty hods downward. In a few minutes, my friend the manager of the plaster company came in. He said, "Mr. Bates, it is all right. We are loading your plaster and we will have it all here before nine o'clock." You may be sure I was relieved.

I went up on the scaffold and watched the men work. I have been in many buildings and had many men in my employ, but I never had men that worked as they did. The plaster went on like grease, and it all stayed where it was put. There seemed to be none falling to the scaffold nor to the floor below. I was on the scaffold part of the time and on the floor part of the time and I don't think a piece of plaster as large as a ten-cent piece fell on my coat. It was on the ceiling.

The lathers were working ahead of the plasterers, and finished about midnight.

By that time we had one coat of plaster on the ceiling and down the side walls to the gallery. The men stopped and ate their lunch, which was provided by Mrs. Bates. They then returned to the scaffold and the second coat was applied. At five o'clock the next morning, it was finished. The contractor said he had never seen anything like it in his life. I am sure I never did, and all the plasterers said the same. They expected it would take them several days to do that work.

When Mrs. Eddy said, "Plaster the church," she provided a way by which it could be done, and there was no time when it was safe to retreat a single inch: no matter what obstacle seemed to be in the way,—what resistance we met, we must press forward and carry out her demonstration. She would [not] have issued that order if she had not known what could have been accomplished; we did not comprehend it until it was finished.

I had not slept for two nights, and consequently, I was very glad to go to my rooms. We locked up the church, leaving a watchman with instructions to admit no person until Monday morning. We sent word to the church services that students were not to be admitted to the church on Sunday, as they had frequently been up to see the progress of the work. We did not wish them there. The Directors did not know of the arrangement I had made for the plastering, nor did they know the church was plastered until Monday morning, when they were relieved and glad to see it.

Some of the students had a way of coming into the church at different times,—frequently just before five o'clock,—looking it over, and making the remark, "You won't get it done, will you?" We felt they should have considered the matter in the light of healing a patient who seemed very sick and perhaps was about to die. They would not go to him and say, "You won't get well, will you?" They would take the affirmative position and be exceedingly agreeable. If the students who knew nothing whatever of mechanical work nor of what was being done there had taken that position, it would have helped us a little. We finally had to close the door on all students and everybody that was not directly connected with the work, because they came in and troubled the workmen, asked them questions which were not important but took their time, an hour of which was very precious.

After plastering the church, there was less opposition to the work, which made it a trifle easier for us until the church was opened for service. This was a relief. But there was much to be done. Early the next week, we applied the finishing coat of plaster in the daytime and then the auditorium was finished as regards that part of the work.

The plastering contractor came to me and said, "Mr. Bates, nothing like this was ever done before to my knowledge. I have never seen nor heard anything like it. It is wonderful that this church was plastered, two coats in twelve hours." As I recall it, nearly all of the journeymen came to me and expressed themselves delighted in having taken part in the work; they said when they went on the scaffold they had no idea that they would get on a single coat through the night,—never thinking of the second coat which was put on. They saw it done, but could not understand how it was done. They applied twenty-four tons of plaster, containing several tons of water, in twelve hours, which to them was incredible. The hod-carriers had a busy time taking up this weight of plaster.

The scaffold was in place and well adapted for the painters' use. The day the plastering was finished, the contractor wished to tear down the scaffold and remove it from the building. Mrs. Bates had a long conversation with him and proposed that he should leave it there ten days or more in order that the painting might be done. At first he demurred, but finally consented when we told him that we would tear it down and put it out of the building without expense to him.

The following Thursday, we commenced to paint the green plaster. The painter demurred and everybody connected with the work objected, saying that it would not do. I held to it that it must do. We must proceed with the painting. I would take the responsibility of its being satisfactory. So the painting was begun. Three coats were applied between that time and the following Thursday, when it was finished.

At seven o'clock that evening, the plasterer came in with two or three of his best men; we had a large corps of volunteer Christian Scientists who were ready to take the scaffold down. This was taken down piece by piece and put out of the windows onto the sidewalk, until it was all removed. Then there remained four thousand feet of boards on the floor which had protected the mosaics. These were also carried out, the sawdust under the temporary floor was removed, the mosaic floor swept clean and in good condition for the contractor for the seats to begin setting them Friday morning. This gave him eight days before the church was to be opened for service, which was sufficient.

It will now be seen that I was right in building the mosaic floor before we plastered, because if the floor had not been built, there would not have been time enough to have built it after the scaffold was removed at the time appointed by Mrs. Eddy for holding the service in the church. So on Friday, the twenty-first, the auditorium was plastered, painted, shaded in colors, the mosaic floor laid, and the principal work to be done was the setting of the seats. We gave the seat contractor all the help he wanted so that this work might progress rapidly. Having laid the concrete and mosaic floor several weeks before, it was like stone and was in an admirable condition to receive bolts for fastening the seats.

A few days previous to this, I had received word to discharge the architect. I simply said, "Yes." It seemed strange to me that a Board should put me in full charge of the work, empower me to employ an architect, and then dictate to me about his discharge, when he was the most necessary person of all to progress the work. During the seven weeks that I was there, he was discharged three times, but he had no knowledge of it except on the first occasion. About the time the plastering was finished, I received word again to discharge him. I said, "Yes." I had made up my mind that I should discharge him—after the church was finished,—which I did. I obeyed, but I did not hasten to obey.

The Marble Arch

The entrance to the Mother's Room which was in the tower of the church was low so that a person must stoop to go through the opening. This was a serious defect. The entrance should be dignified and in keeping with the uses of the room. We consulted our architect and decided to build a marble arch facing the main vestibule. He designed a beautiful structure and it was submitted to the parties in Baltimore who had the contract for all the other marble work in the church; they were a reliable firm with facilities for getting out work rapidly, and they had the stock on hand. There was no time to lose, and we requested them to name a price for the work set up, and limited them as to time, which limit they accepted and fulfilled. Transportation was good then and reliable. Steamers ran directly from Baltimore to Boston, occupying only about two days in transit; and the marble was loaded on, packed securely, delivered in Boston, and taken to the church within two weeks after the order was given.

In order to prepare for the arch, it was necessary to cut out quite an amount of masonry, which raised a strong protest from the builders and others. I knew that it could be done; I consulted experts regarding it, and we decided that it was perfectly feasible. A series of heavy steel beams were made and placed in position before any other cutting was done; they were keyed up so that they carried the weight of that part of the tower, which some said would fall down if we disturbed the mason work as it had been built. We made these beams extra strong, however, with a large factor of safety, and there has never been any difficulty arising from it. We then cut out the head of the door to the height we wanted to place the arch.

The men were in the building, and the setting up of the upright parts to support the arch was begun immediately on the arrival of the marble. It was desirable that this arch should be finished, as several other kinds of mechanical work were dependent upon its completion. After the uprights had been set up (mechanics had worked at it about four days), I asked the foreman how long it would take to finish the arch. He said about four days more. I asked him if he was willing to work that night. He answered he was, and his men would work with him and do all they could. We detailed two Scientists to remain there and help them all they could mentally. The work progressed nicely, was carefully fitted and finished, and at eight o'clock the following morning it was complete, which was a great satisfaction to all concerned. It is a beautiful piece of work and has been complimented very highly by artists and people who have traveled abroad and seen some of the best work in Europe.

Mrs. Bates, in her paper, has described the finishing of the tower, which was a very important matter. By doing what we did, we obeyed Mrs. Eddy and the difficulties all vanished before obedience, as they will. I, myself, did not see this part of the work completed and did not know what Mrs. Bates was doing, as I had plenty of work in the auditorium. Most of the time, while I was there, I had two hundred or more men working at twenty trades, and I was busy every moment. Questions were coming up constantly and adjustments had to be made and must be instantly decided; there was no time to lose. Doorways from the auditorium to the vestibule were not of an even height. Very little about the building was correct in dimension and proportion and did not correspond with the plans. Much revision and adjustment was required as the different tradesmen arrived at the point of completing their work. It seemed that everything that could be crooked was crooked; but it was all made straight in due time.

Bronze Window Frames

The window frames designed for the various windows were of heavy plank and filled up the opening from four to six inches. The window space, as designed, was rather small for lighting the church, when we take into consideration that most of the glass was colored and did not admit the full light. It seemed desirable to eliminate these thick frames and add twenty percent, or possibly more, to the effective lighting of the church. This was finally done and a bronze frame was substituted, only half an inch thick, which added very much to the appearance of the church because it was less conspicuous than window frames, and enhanced the effect of the figures and decorations by giving additional space.

It might be well to state here that Mrs. Eddy

sent a messenger from her home with letters—sometimes to me, sometimes to Mrs. Bates, sometimes to the Directors, and at other times to us all. These letters came daily or two or three times a week, as the occasion for them arose in her mind. The letters usually inquired how the work was progressing, what part of the building or what class of the work occupied us, and made some recommendation or suggestion, or gave definite command as to what should be done.

She also requested that we each write her, from our own standpoint, about the work we were doing, and we sent the letters by the same messenger. It may seem strange that Mrs. Eddy sent one of her own household with the letters, which she often wrote early in the morning or during the night, the messenger taking the first train from Concord. She found that letters sent by mail were sometimes tampered with, and we learned afterwards that there was a spy in the Concord post office. She then tried the express company, and her letters were either not delivered promptly or had been opened before delivery. This being the case, she had no recourse but to put them in the hands of a person in her own household who could be trusted and would deliver the letters to the person addressed.

Mrs. Eddy's letters were at times a source of mystery to us, and not until the church was finished and dedicated and we had time to realize what they meant, did their full import occur to us. We then knew that, day by day as the work progressed, Mrs. Eddy was demonstrating at her home in Concord and our whole duty was to obey; when we did obey the work progressed rapidly,—so rapidly that it seemed as though, when we commenced a piece of work, it was done. And so, little by little, we learned to do what seemed to be impossible; it was proven to be very possible under her demonstration.

The Church Roof

From the time we first went into the church to take charge of the work, there was always a question about the progress of the roof, which was very unsatisfactory. Upon inquiry, we found that its construction had been going on for months with no sign of immediate completion. Upon inquiring the reason why, various statements were made, among which was that the workmen wouldn't work on the roof. Experienced roofers would go on the roof at eight o'clock in the morning and come down at ten or eleven, quaking with fear, saying they wouldn't work on the building. Other men were employed and sent up and would leave the work, making the same excuse, till finally it seemed to be almost impossible to get anyone who would go on the roof. The weather was extremely bad,— cold, windy and stormy most of the time; but there were a few days when conditions were better, although the cold continued to be severe nearly every day. After the terra cotta had been placed between the iron rafters and tarred roofing felt spread over it, which partially protected the auditorium, men were sent up to slate the roof, put in copper gutters, and do all that class of work which was necessary; but they would not remain on the roof.

There must be a cause for this, and one day, in conversation with one of the Directors, we asked who the contractor was. He told us, and Mrs. Bates said at once, "I want to see him."

He said, "He is on the roof and he will be coming down the ladder in a few minutes," which he did.

As he came down the ladder, Mrs. Bates said quietly, "He is a Spiritualist,—that is what is the matter with the roof."

The other parties said, "No, I don't believe it."

She affirmed that it was so. When he came to the ground there was a little quiet talk about Spiritualism and he joined in with avidity and said he had seances in his house and was proud of the fact; he said, "Spiritualism was just as good as Christian Science and was about the same thing."

We did not talk with him long, but retired. The matter was handled scientifically and in a day or two there was a good gang of men on the roof who worked with as much comfort as roofers can in cold weather; we had the satisfaction of seeing the building housed in rapidly, and it was finished before we had a service in the church, much to our relief, and much to the relief of all the contractors, since we had, as before stated, laid in the mosaic floor, put up the mosaic dado, plastered the ceiling, painted it, and had made various decorations that needed protection.

The Final Touches

Saturday, the twenty-ninth, was a busy day, as all the preceeding ones had been. There seemed to be an enormous amount of work to be done to have service there on the day following, but we were not the army of retreat. One in Concord was demonstrating and we felt the support of this; the word was "to go forward." At four o'clock that afternoon the last stone was laid, which was the keystone of the arch over the entrance to the lower vestibule. This completed the exterior of the building.

At five o'clock that afternoon, an immense amount of work had been done; but there remained about a hundred and fifty days' work to be done before we could comfortably occupy the auditorium. Our negative friends came in and said, "You won't get it done, will you?" Other doubting Thomases were plenty. Very few people had anything encouraging to say. There were some who believed it could be done and offered willing hands to help us, which we gladly accepted.

Most of the contractors were kindly disposed and willing to do anything that we asked; they would work overtime if we requested it. But one contractor had been sexton of a church,—a man with a very moderate education, who wore a clerical robe buttoned high in the throat, and dragged on his heels, who never did anything to forward the work if he could avoid it. His theology would not permit him to do so. All of his workmen reflected his thought, and it was very difficult to get along with them. At five o'clock his men locked up the tools and were leaving the building. I went to them and asked them if they would not work overtime,—we would pay them liberally; we had a few things to do in their line and it was very necessary to finish their work before the service in the morning. They flatly refused; neither arguments nor money availed. I said to one of them, "Won't you give us the key to your tool box?"

He said, "No," put it in his pocket, and went out of the building.

This left us in a peculiar position. For several days we had been getting the windows in the church and had them all in except the window representing, "The Woman God Crowned," which, as you face it, is at the right of the organ. This window sat on the floor. At first it seemed our services would be held without the window in place, but reason and Science came to the rescue. We went to the tool box without a key and it yielded to our persuasions. We selected the necessary tools and my own foreman, who was in the building, did the work of preparing for the window and fastening it in place; this occupied him until twelve o'clock that night, but it was done. That finished the windows.

It might be well to say that upon making a personal inspection of the said tool box, we found that all the hinges on it were loose and it was an easy matter to get the tools. After the window was set, we put back the tools, pressed the hinges in their places without fastening them, and left the box as we found it.

At five o'clock that evening, viewing the room there appeared about a hundred and fifty days' work to be done before occupying the auditorium, but this did not stagger me. We had many mechanics there, representing all the different trades, who were willing helpers, and together with them, we had many Scientists,—ladies and gentlemen who came in to dust, clean and do anything they could to make ready for the opening of the church. The work went on quietly but rapidly. The clock struck twelve. In looking about the auditorium floor and gallery, I noticed a great procession of men and women walking towards the vestibule. I was surprised. Every person in that room finished his work at the same moment. There were cleaners, masons, carpenters, brick layers, electricians, and so on,—all manner of work going on, and all finished and went to the stairways to place their tools in the lower vestry at the same moment,— for the work was done and the room was ready for occupancy.

Mrs. Eddy said, "Have the room ready in December." As the clock tolled the hour of midnight, everything was done; we could all go home to return to a service early in the morning, which we enjoyed exceedingly. Mrs. Eddy's demonstration was complete to the minute. We had enjoyed seeing it and were educated by it. I did not realize this so much at the time, except that I was rejoiced that it was done and was satisfied; but years afterwards it came to me— the picture of that procession walking by unanimous consent to put away their tools and implements which they had used in finishing the room. Nothing was said; no one said, "Time is up;" voluntarily they took their course and laid their tools away. I shall never forget the panorama which presented itself before me. I shall never forget the lesson of precision that it taught me. It was worth all the weeks that I had spent in Boston.

Many of the ladies who helped clean the church and prepare for the service had come from the suburban districts and brought their Sunday clothes with them, intending to stay. It was late to go to a hotel, the weather was unpropitious and on Christmas Day we had bought the building known as 95 Falmouth Street (which was for the Publishing House and was used for that purpose soon after the dedication of the church). We put one bed in there which Mrs. Bates and I occupied, and we gave up our rooms on Huntington Avenue to Mr. and Mrs. Kimball who came on to be present at the opening service of the church. Some of these ladies found friends with whom they could remain; others slept on the floor of the Publishing House so as to be there early to go to church. Their heart was in the work and they were excellent helpers. The white mahogany furniture in the Mother's Room was also in the building. Our experience taught us that the old proverb should be in mind that, "A bird in the hand was worth two in the bush." We had this furniture made and delivered several days before, to be sure that it was ready to place in the Mother's Room before the church was dedicated, and it was wise that we did so. We tried to cover every point, and prepare for every contingency.

Sunday morning before the first service, two noted theosophists came into the church, went into the gallery, and looking about the auditorium, said to one of the ushers, "When did you finish the inside of this church? We have been watching the outside and noticed its incomplete condition, especially the roof, and had no idea that you had finished the interior of the building." They seemed almost amazed that it could be done, but their utterance gave us a point for further use. We afterwards learned they had leased a suite of rooms within a few hundred feet of the church, so located that they could sit at their study-window and watch the progress of the building.

The week between the opening service and the dedication, which occurred on the sixth day of January, 1895, the Sunday of the Epiphany, was a busy week finishing details and getting everything in order for the reception of the many students coming from all parts of the United States who had signified their intention of being present.

Mrs. Eddy wrote the dedicatory sermon, which was afterwards published freely and can be found in her book Pulpit and Press. There was diligent search for a proper person to read this address, and a lady was finally selected who proved to be very competent and read it to the great satisfaction of the audiences.

Five services were held which about six thousand students attended, and the church was formally dedicated to the service of God.

In another week, most of the details about the church were taken care of, and I was invited to visit Mrs. Eddy at her home, Pleasant View, Concord, New Hampshire, on the fifteenth of January. I had not seen her since the summer before. Mrs. Bates had been called up there several times on business matters, but I was so busy in the church I could not get away, and the word was to apply ourselves to the finishing of the building.

I very joyfully accepted Mrs. Eddy's invitation to spend a day with her, and took an early train for Concord. On my arrival, she met me in the library and asked me many questions about the church and how we proceeded to overcome the difficulties and prepare it for service on the twenty-ninth of December. She showed a great deal of interest in every detail. But finally a sad expression came over her countenance and she said, "Six thousand of my students could be there and enjoy the services and dedication of the church. Several members of my household went down, but I was not invited." This gave me quite a shock, as I supposed the invitation to our teacher had been given either by the Directors or by the First Members. I had not been able to attend the meetings of either of these bodies because my time was so thoroughly taken up in the edifice. It seemed to me a great oversight to leave the Discoverer and Founder of Christian Science alone in her home while thousands of students were enjoying themselves meeting in the edifice.

Dinner was duly served and while at dinner, she stopped eating and said, "Mr. Bates, the Directors were up here yesterday and I told them that, but for you, the church would never have been built."

I replied, "Mrs. Eddy, but for you the church would never have been built."

She said again, "Mr. Bates, but for you the church would never have been built."

I again replied, "But for you, Mrs. Eddy, the church never would have been built."

The third time she said, "Mr. Bates, if you had not come and helped me, the church never would have been built."

I replied, "Mrs. Eddy, but for your demonstrations the church would never have been built." There was no further conversation of this nature at the table, and after dinner we retired again to the library and were alone for some time.

After a general conversation, she looked me straight in the eye and said, "Mr. Bates, are you prepared for what is to come?" I could not think what she meant, and asked her. She said, "Are you prepared for the treatment you will receive?" I could not imagine what she meant. I supposed that everybody would be so glad the church was built and we could hold services in our own temple that they would rejoice with everyone who had anything to do with its construction. She went on to say, "You came here in answer to prayer. I prayed God for three months to send me a man to finish the church. He heard my prayer and sent you and you followed my demonstration and the church is finished;—but they will hate you for helping Mother." This seemed incomprehensible. She went on to say, "They will shun you; they will try to ruin you morally, physically, financially and spiritually." Of this I had ample proof within a few weeks.

I remained there until time to take the evening train, after a most pleasant interview; Mrs. Eddy gave me a great many points to think about.

Before my leaving, she said, "We have built the church; it will be easy for branch churches to build their structures as we have cleared the way. If The Mother Church had not been finished at the time I designated, it would have remained a monument to the error and my students would have died sudden and unnatural deaths. You have helped me to save them."

The Invitation

When Mrs. Eddy told me that she was not invited to the dedication, I determined to send her an invitation to visit the church which she had built. Consequently, I composed an invitation and took it to a jeweler to advise with him as to the preferable form. We finally decided we would engrave it on a scroll which he designed. This seemed very appropriate and it was made. The scroll was enclosed in a suitable casket appropriate for its reception.

A few days later, Mrs. Bates and I went to Concord bearing this casket in our hands and carried it to the house. When we arrived there, Mrs. Eddy was out taking her usual drive, but we told the attendant the nature of our errand and the casket was placed on the library table and opened and the scroll set at a proper angle for reading. The attendant asked us to sit in the parlor until Mrs. Eddy returned and ascertain if she wished to see us and what she would have to say.

We remained in the parlor perhaps half an hour and Mrs. Eddy returned. The attendant invited her into the library and said, "Look at that, Mrs. Eddy." We were not present, but we understood that Mrs. Eddy read the invitation and was overcome by her feelings. After a few minutes, she said, "Are they here?"

The attendant answered we were in the parlor.

She said, "Invite them in." As we entered the library, Mrs. Eddy embraced Mrs. Bates and wept on her neck. Afterwards, she took me by the hand and laid her head on my shoulder and said nothing. When she recovered her composure, she went to the table, and, looking at the invitation, she said, "Who wrote it, Mr. Bates?"

I replied, "I did."

She asked no more questions, but said, "You put

me in my proper place. You seem to know who I am and what I deserve."

(From *People and Patriot*, Concord, New Hampshire. February twenty-seven, 1895)

"Magnificent Testimonial"

"Members of the First Church of Christ, Scientist, at Boston, have forwarded to Mrs. Mary Baker Eddy of this city, the founder of Christian Science, a Testimonial which is probably one of the most magnificent examples of the goldsmith's art ever wrought in this country. It is in the form of a gold scroll, twenty-six inches long, nine inches wide, and an eighth of an inch thick.

"It bears upon its face the following inscription cut in script letters:

'Dear Mother,

'During the year 1894, a church edifice was erected at the intersection of Falmouth and Norway streets in the city of Boston by the loving hands of four thousand members. This edifice is built as a Testimonial to truth as revealed by divine Love through you to this age. You are hereby most lovingly invited to visit and formally accept this testimonial on the 20th day of February, 1895, at high noon.

'The First Church of Christ, Scientist, at Boston, Mass.

'To the Reverend Mary Baker Eddy,

'By Edward P. Bates

'Boston, January 6, 1895 Caroline S. Bates'

"Attached by a white ribbon to the scroll is a gold key to the Mother's Room. The testimonial is encased in a white satin lined box of rich green velvet."

We returned to Boston and the next day to Syracuse, little dreaming that the matter would have any great publicity. But after being in Syracuse two or three days, we received communication from a student in Boston with clippings from the Concord and Boston papers. It seemed that Mrs. Eddy had sent the invitation to be placed on exhibition in the window of a prominent jeweler's store on State Street, in Concord, where the people of her resident city might read it. When the articles came out in the newspapers, there was a great stir among the students in Boston and they said a good many things. The most striking of them was that we had no right to invite Mrs. Eddy to the church. When I read this I said, "Mrs. Eddy was not invited by those who should have invited her. I took the responsibility of doing so. I wrote the invitation and presented it to her. She accepted the invitation and that is all there is to it."

Mrs. Eddy published the invitation and some of the newspaper comments on pages 112 to 115, inclusive, of her book, *Pulpit and Press*, which she issued soon after the church was dedicated. [pp.76-78 in current edition]

Mrs. Eddy came to the church the first day of April of that year and occupied the Mother's Room. After removing her outer garments, she went into the auditorium through the door nearest Norway Street and knelt down for several minutes. What she said was only known to herself and God. I did not see this, but a faithful student who was present saw her kneel and left the room. Afterwards she looked about the auditorium and expressed herself very much pleased with its restful air. (This was the intention always in selecting colors.) She made one comment at that time and at other times, that the auditorium was not large enough for the people who would wish to come and hear the Bible and Science and Health read together. She had hoped that the church would seat fifteen hundred, but it would seat about eleven hundred. She immediately said, "We will soon have to build a larger church." This was provided for in the extension of The Mother Church ten years later, which seats over five thousand people comfortably.

Mrs. Eddy called us to her residence frequently about these times and asked me to take a position on the Board of Directors, which I did a few weeks later. She also appointed me President of the Church, which position I held four different terms.

The visits to Pleasant View were very much to our benefit and for the benefit of the Publishing Society and the church work in general. There was a question about Sunday school lessons,— whether we would continue to use the International Series or not; and it was decided that we would use the subject of the International Series, but that in teaching, it should be illustrated by the light of Christian Science. Later she gave us subjects for the lessons, which subjects have been used continually from that time until this, very much to the advantage of The Mother Church and all the branch churches and societies.

It was about this time that some Normal students told me that Mrs. Eddy taught them differently from any other class she taught. The class they were in was very high in spiritual attainment and Mrs. Eddy could carry them up above other classes. I refuted this immediately. First, because Mrs. Eddy had told me that she had never had a class prepared as a whole to take her teaching. There might be some members in it which she could have taken to a high spiritual plane, provided she had not been obliged to teach other students the rudiments of Christian Science, thus holding back the class. She said she would like to have before her a class of students who were qualified to take her teaching. I also told these students who made the statement that Mrs. Eddy was consistent. Mine had been the privilege of sitting in three classes and I knew what she taught. I also had hundreds of interviews with her since the first class I attended and listened to her teaching, and she always talked on one line,—that is, "Recapitulation." She used this for her text in the class and tried to bring the students up to the spiritual conception of its meaning. She also did the same in her private conversations with her students,—always trying to unfold to us in Science what would be to our spiritual benefit. It was a constant unfolding.

I well remember, after sitting in her first class, that I immediately read the several Epistles in the New Testament, and I found I had a new book in my hand. An illumination came to me I had never conceived possible. My previous reading had been under the hypnotism of old theology with the bondage of its rules of what you must believe and what you must not believe, according to its way of interpreting it; when this hypnotic spell was broken by her teaching, I was free. The veil was lifted from the truth and I could read and understand what I read. Consequently, I loved the Bible more than ever before. After the Quarterlies were established, the study of the Bible, by the aid of the Quarterlies, has been exceedingly interesting and beneficial.

Another point which was talked of during our interview with Mrs. Eddy was the Friday evening meetings, as they were started first on that evening and continued for a few weeks, then were changed to Wednesday evenings. She asked me what we did at those meetings and what we talked about. I replied that we usually gave testimonies about healing. She said, "You older students should take up the business of the church and help the younger students to understand it. These meetings are for this purpose as well as for testimonies for the healing."

Through the spring and summer of 1895, Mrs. Eddy frequently gave me commissions to execute in Boston. She would say, "See the older students and ask them to do certain things."

I replied, "Yes, shall I tell them it is your request?"

She replied, "No! Do not mention my name."

I replied, it would seem as though I were directing their conduct, and I felt it inadvisable for me to take that position; but she insisted that I should do as she told me, which I did. This occurred on several occasions and the message was taken correctly, as I knew how to deliver it. Most of the students rebelled at what they thought was a piece of impertinence on my part, and I could say nothing more than to deliver the message and let it rest there.

It was during the month of March that I began to realize what Mrs. Eddy meant when she said, "The students will shun you," *et cetera.* I found, in an audience of over one thousand students, there were hardly fifteen or twenty of them that would speak to me at all, and many of them took deliberate pains to shun my personality. It went about the church currently that the Bateses were animal magnetism and that if people wanted to be well and live, they must shun the Bateses. Mrs. Eddy never wrote nor taught that any one person or any one set of persons embodied animal magnetism. We bore this as well as we could, but it continued with gradually less pressure until I was appointed President of the church for the third term, when it nearly died out. I remember well that many students came to me and took my hand, saying that they had been abusing me both orally and mentally and wanted to be forgiven. I told them that I had nothing against them and was glad if they wanted to do right instead of wrong.

385 Commonwealth Avenue

Mrs. Eddy said when she bought the above mentioned house, it was to be the Pastor's residence; she looked upon the office of the First Reader as being similar to that of pastor, and she desired to provide a good home for the First Reader. After living in the house two or three years, she moved to Concord, New Hampshire.

In the spring of 1895, she sent for me and commissioned me to do considerable work on the house. It was in a block and looked like the other houses; she wished to have it emphasized in some way so that it might be distinguished from the others. It was located near the middle of the block, so this could be done to advantage. The vestibule doors of the house were red oak, hardly in keeping with the style of the building. The vestibule itself was very plain and was susceptible of improvement. She also suggested building a room or tower on the roof which could be seen for several blocks, and the house put in general good order.

We employed the same architect who helped us finish the church; he made designs and specifications for the remodeling of parts of the house, for additions and renovations, submitted them to her, and she ordered the work done and the bills brought to her when it was finished. I employed the same builder who was so efficient in finishing The Mother Church, and set him at work. We removed the front and the vestibule doors and substituted very fine San Domingo mahogany doors with panels of cathedral glass. The hardware for the original doors was common, and we had elegant bronze fittings made for the new doors. A very neat design in mosaics was made for the floor of the vestibule, which was laid, also dado on the sides. This very much improved the appearance of the front. The room which was built on the roof had slightly the appearance of a tower, with a stairway leading up to it, and it was a very nice apartment to retire to on a summer evening, and it distinguished the house from its neighbors.

The entire house was renovated, the work being done according to her direction, at a cost of several thousand dollars, and she appeared well satisfied with it. I remember, when she was in Boston in October, she wished to drive by the house and look at it, which she did; Mrs. Bates and myself accompanied her, and she expressed herself as very much pleased with the change. She felt satisfied that it was a dignified and serviceable home for the First Reader of the Church.

In the summer of 1895, Mrs. Eddy frequently called the First Members to her residence,— sometimes all of them, and sometimes a portion of them. It was during one of these visits that she gave us very careful instructions on many points which we needed. She always insisted on taking up brotherly love and tried to instill the necessity of demonstrating this virtue between ourselves.

One day, I remember, she paused suddenly and said, "What is the matter with Mr. Bates? You told me that if Mr. Bates paid his debts he would not have a dollar in the world. I wanted to know the truth about this statement for myself, and I informed myself through the Syracuse banks. They tell me that Mr. Bates is worth seventy-five thousand dollars or more and is in high credit. I think this is pretty good for a young man who has only been in business for a few years." The whole thing was a great surprise to me, but I knew from what she said that the report made to her was stated as a fact, and she wished to kill it.

Mrs. Eddy was constantly taking thought for her students. If a student said something wrong about another student, she often brought them together, went over the matter and corrected it in the presence of both, and thus killed the error. She also received many letters from various students about some of her best workers. She always managed to let the worker know what was claimed against him and if he had been injudicious in any matter, he could correct it; if it was a lie, he could protect himself mentally against the lies. She was good to us all, trying to keep us working in harmony and thinking well of the other person,—never thinking maliciously of anyone who told a wrong thing about us.

The Invitation to Pleasant View

The Annual Meeting was held the latter part of June, 1895, and a large number of students were remaining over for the Sunday service. On Friday, the second of July, Mrs. Eddy invited the members of the church to come to Pleasant View on Monday, the fifth, and she requested me to prepare trains for their transportation. I received this message late Friday afternoon.

Early Saturday morning I went to the general ticket office of the Boston and Maine Railroad to arrange for transportation. They asked me how many would go and I told them about twelve hundred. They said they would have to print a special half-fare ticket, and that we could have the tickets at eight o'clock Monday morning; they would send out a train at nine o'clock and a second would follow at nine-fifteen, twelve cars each. I asked how we would sell the tickets. They shrugged their shoulders and said they did not know. I asked the ticket seller how long it would take to sell twelve hundred tickets. He said he could sell them in three hours provided he did not have any other trains to look after, but he always had a great many trains. Here was a conundrum: the invitation to Concord and no tickets till eight o'clock Monday morning, and the train leaving at nine! I did a good deal of thinking. I remember Sunday evening as I sat in our sitting-room I was very quiet for a couple of hours. We had several Science friends there, some who were stopping with us over the Sunday service and were going on the excursion. I was asked why I did not take part in the conversation. I replied I had plenty to think about. I had become satisfied that if Mrs. Eddy asked us to do something, there was a way to do it and a right way, and that we could find the way.

I finally thought out a plan for handling the tickets. We would not trouble the ticket sellers but would frame a little booth in the midway and sell our own tickets. In bunches of five, we could sell them for eight dollars, the buyer making the change.

At eight o'clock, I had five bank cashiers on the ground to handle the money, five other gentlemen to hand out the tickets, and six or eight to pass the tickets to the students,—no student coming within two yards of the booth, but passing up the money to the intermediate person; they handed it to the persons handling the tickets, and they in turn handed it to the cashiers. Every few minutes I carried four or five hundred dollars to the ticket office and returned with a large bunch of tickets. Two persons in the ticket office were bunching the tickets in packages of five. At eight-forty we had sold nearly all of the tickets for both trains and the passengers were all seated and the first section departed exactly at nine o'clock. Few tickets were sold later, and the second section left at nine-fifteen.

The booth was cleared away, the tickets were paid for, and a few extra tickets were on each train for persons who might have boarded the train without them. I think there were only two tickets sold on the train.

The conductors on both trains expressed to everyone their surprise and satisfaction at our way of handling the holiday excursion. "Everyone had tickets," they said. "All we needed to do was to gather them up. It was the best crowd and the easiest excursion we ever looked after."

Everyone was happy, no one was hurried, everything was done decently and in order. We made a pleasant trip to Concord on one of the hottest days I ever saw anywhere, the thermometer registering one hundred and ten at Concord. There were various carriages at hand, carry-alls came up from Manchester and other cities, so that quite a proportion of the students could ride to Pleasant View; many chose to walk.

We arrived there duly. With our arrival, a great host came in from New Hampshire and Vermont and northern Massachusetts,—by train, by carriage and by any other vehicle they could travel in; it was estimated there were over three thousand people on Mrs. Eddy's lawn.

I know I was trying to clean myself of the smoke and dust when I was told Mrs. Eddy wanted to see me. I met her in the front hall. She said, "Mr.

Bates, take me out and introduce me." I was very much surprised as I supposed different arrangements had been made. The Mayor of Concord was there and several notable gentlemen; General Bates and others among her students, many of national celebrity; I introduced Mrs. Eddy in a few simple words. She gave a mother's message to her students in tenderest terms, overflowing with love, and welcomed them to her home. As many of us know, Mrs. Eddy's house is located several hundred feet back from the road; in conversation with persons who could get no nearer than the front fence, they said they heard every word Mrs. Eddy uttered. Her voice was not loud, but it was absolutely clear and carried well.

The excursion was a success in every way. Thousands of people who had never seen Mrs. Eddy's face before saw it that day and heard her voice, which was a blessing to them. Others who had seen her and known her well, were equally grateful for the privilege.

The Hall at Concord

Soon after the completion of The Mother Church, Mrs. Eddy purchased a house with a large plot of ground at the corner of State Street and the park green in Concord, the second floor of which she immediately converted into a hall where the Concord students could hold church services. When this hall was completed,—it was ready in two or three weeks,—the First Members were invited from Boston to attend the Sunday morning service there.

Mrs. Eddy telegraphed the Friday before, sending the invitation to the First Members. Saturday noon I was called into the Clerk's office and told that, as a First Member, I was invited with the others to attend church in Concord the following morning; but as it was impossible to obtain a train, owing to the rulings of the railroad commission regarding extra Sunday trains, the Clerk had wired Mrs. Eddy that we could not come. I was shocked. I said, "If Mrs. Eddy has invited us, there is a way to go."

"Well," he replied, "try it, if you can get a train. I have been down to the Boston and Maine office and the railroad commission, and they will not let an extra train leave Boston, Sunday morning, and there is no train leaving by which we could get there, til noon or later." I told him if he would put the matter in my charge, I would see what could be done.

I started out on what appeared to be a forlorn hope, but I believed that Mrs. Eddy's wishes could be carried out, and worked on that line. I went to the offices of the railroad commission. It was closed for the Saturday half-holiday. I went to other offices and they were closed for the same reason. I finally entered the general ticket office of the Boston and Maine Railroad, where I was very well known and well received. In fact, after getting up the excursion for twelve hundred on July fifth, I was in great favor with the ticket department, and they had offered several times to do anything for me they could.

When I entered the room the ticket agent smiled. He said, "Your friend has been down here before you."

I said, "Yes."

"Did he tell you what we told him?"

"Yes," I said, "but that has nothing to do with the case."

"Well," he said, "there is a ruling of the railroad commission. If we send out a train, we are liable to several hundred dollars fine, and we can't do it."

I told him I thought we could do it, and we talked perhaps over an hour. Finally I saw that there was some relenting on his part and took advantage of it. He ended by saying, "You want a Pullman car train, don't you?"

"Yes."

"Well," he said, "go over to the Pullman office and see what they will do. If they will give you the cars, perhaps we can arrange it."

I went to the Pullman Company's office and engaged the cars we needed, came back and had another talk with the ticket agent. He finally agreed to give me the train for nine o'clock in the morning.

I hastened to the Clerk, reporting that I had secured the train, and immediately we proceeded to telegraph the Members at Providence, New York, Brooklyn, Long Branch, Buffalo, and telephone those who lived in the vicinity of Boston, which was all quickly done. I telegraphed Mrs. Eddy we would come.

We were at the hall on time. Dr. Frye, Mrs. Eddy's private secretary, met me as I entered and said, "You did well to get here. We received the telegram yesterday noon and were very much disappointed. Mrs. Eddy likes to have people accept her invitations, and when we received your telegram later, we knew that you would come." In a few minutes he said, "Mrs. Eddy wishes you would take her up into the hall," which I did, where she delivered a beautiful exposition of the Ninety-first Psalm. This was, for us, a memorable occasion.

The Afternoon Excursion

A few weeks later, Mrs. Eddy invited the First Members to come to the Christian Science Hall in Concord and meet her there. This being a week day, trains were running regularly and there was no difficulty in getting a train for our purpose, although we had a special. We were so overjoyed at the thought of meeting our teacher and passing an hour with her that we were probably careless, and not demonstrating as we should. Between Nashua and Manchester we found a freight train derailed in such a way as to block our passage. Then we began to realize our heedlessness, and to work in the right direction. Mrs. Eddy was wired of the delay of the train; after waiting about an hour we proceeded and reached Concord an hour late.

We entered the building and Dr. Frye said to me and others, "Mrs. Eddy was not coming to the Hall this afternoon as your late arrival interfered with her plans, but she is here." We were invited up to the Hall and Mrs. Eddy sat on the rostrum and welcomed us. She also told us that if we did not make a better demonstration next time, we need not come.

Mrs. Eddy talked a while, and then paused and resumed, "I want to hear you talk. When you come to see me, I do all the talking. When I meet you in public, I do all the talking. Now I want to hear my students talk." I suppose they all felt as I did,—that to talk to Mrs. Eddy in a public place was a very serious thing, consequently, we were silent. After a few moments of silence, she called on two or three of the students and asked them some questions which they answered briefly. Finally she said, "This meeting is not taking the right course. I invited you up here to listen to what you have to say to me, and I hear nothing from you. I will tell you a story, 'A little girl had a kitten. She was a devout Baptist and was taught to believe that immersion was necessary to salvation. She did not want her kitten to be lost, so one day she drew the bathtub half full of water and attempted to immerse it. The kitten, having strong objections, scratched the little girl's hand and got away. She caught it and tried it again, with similar results. The third time she caught the kitten and tried to immerse it, with like results. She looked at the kitten in a hopeless way. She said, 'Be a 'Piscopal kitten and go to hell if you want to.' Now," she said, "let's talk in a social way." So the conversation was carried on until the time arrived for us to return to Boston.

Mrs. Eddy loved a good story and could tell it with a flourish. I remember one day when I went to her house she said, "Mr. Bates, did you know I had bought the lot adjoining mine on the east?"

I said, "I heard something about it."

"Yes," she said, "I have bought it and I have the deed. I want to tell you how I got it. It is a tumbled down old place not worth anything; decaying apple trees, burdocks, tin cans and old chicken coops, and a general dilapidation. I pass it every day on my afternoon drive, and if I could buy it for what it was worth, I desired to clean it up, tear down the house, cut down the trees which were dead, and fill the lot somewhat and add it to my lawn. So I started, as I afterwards learned, on the wrong plan. I sent for the owner of the house and asked him his price. He said, 'Miss Eddy, I don't know. I'll have to ask So-and-So down to the city.' 'Well, when you find out what it is worth, come and see me.' 'I will, Miss Eddy.' He called on his spiritual adviser in Concord. He said, 'Miss Eddy wants to buy my house and lot. How much shall I ask her?' 'Well, Bill, now that's a pretty good house of yourn—it's worth six hundred dollars, and the lot is worth a thousand,' said he, 'I would ask her sixteen hundred dollars for it.' 'All right, Jim.' And he called on me and reported. 'Miss Eddy,' he said, 'that house and lot of mine is worth sixteen hundred dollars.' 'Well, how do you make that out?' 'I have been to see Jim So-and-So and he says the house is worth six hundred dollars and the lot is worth a thousand.' I said, 'I don't care to buy it.'"

She waited a year and concluded she had started at the wrong end of the matter, so she sent for the spiritual adviser and told him that she would be glad to buy the house and lot next to hers if she could buy it for what it was worth. Said he, "All right, Mrs. Eddy; I think I can buy it for you."

"If you do," she said, "I will give you a valuable present."

So he called on the owner and said, "Bill, Mrs. Eddy wants that house and lot of yours. I think you might as well let her have it. I guess she will give you about what it is worth. That house ain't worth anything really, and that lot is worth about six hundred dollars." Said he, "I would let her have it for six hundred dollars if I was you."

"All right, if you think that is what it is worth, I will let her have it."

"Well, come down town," he said, "and make out the deed;" so they did and the spiritual adviser went to see Mrs. Eddy. "Here is your deed, Mrs. Eddy."

She read it over; it seemed to be worded right, and she put it into the pocket of her dress (an appendage which she always had). She said, "Thank you," and started to leave the room.

"Mrs. Eddy, Mrs. Eddy, you said if I would buy that house and lot for you, you would give me a valuable present."

"Oh, I did, did I? Well, I will give you the house."

"But," he said, "that house ain't worth anything."

"Well, you said it was worth six hundred dollars,—I am sure that is a big price for buying me the house and lot."

"Now, Mrs. Eddy," he said, "that house ain't

worth anything and you promised me a valuable present." After chaffing him a few minutes, she gave him a round fee for doing the business.

While she was telling me this story, her eyes glistened, bright as diamonds, and her whole face was radiant with fun. It was grand to see her in this frame of mind; we usually found her burdened with serious things, the care of her students and the conversion of the world. How to proceed, with her, was always a mooted question. She often said she was never permitted to do what she called "the ultimate right," but always had to choose the least of two evils on account of the existing conditions. It seemed strange to me that the Discoverer and Founder of Christian Science could not do right when she knew what was right, but I afterwards realized it was discretion; that she must raise her students to her level before she could give them the ultimate right.

At one time she was looking out of the window,— a fresh breeze was blowing across the lawn, and the grass, some inches high, was bending to the breeze. She said, "I am like that grass you see bending before the breeze,—I never resist it—I bend with it—it blows over and is gone, then I straighten up like the grass."

At another time, while there, a thunder storm was gathering and the clouds were very dense. She looked out of the window, noticed it, and in ten minutes the sky was clear. She said, "I can stop its raining any time, but I can't make it rain." A person will need to read the second chapter of Genesis very carefully to understand what she meant.

From time to time as we were called to her home either singly or in company with others, she took the occasion of giving us instructions as to our course of action, and all this instruction was exceedingly valuable.

The Second Visit to The Mother Church

The second and last visit Mrs. Eddy made to The Mother Church was early in October, 1895. She came to the city in a private car on Saturday and spent the night in her room. In order to utilize her time, at her request several of her students visited her Saturday night, one following the other in succession, and she gave them splendid instructions as to the course to pursue in their work. Sunday morning as the hour arrived for service, we had everything prepared for Mrs. Eddy to go down the aisle on the Falmouth Street side and enter the platform by the door under the choir gallery. I was told who was to introduce her, and merely stood by the door to open it when she should appear. For some reason which I did not know, as she came out of the Mother's Room she said, "Mr. Bates, you are to take me in," which I did. As we went down the aisle the students all rose as a mark of courtesy and remained standing until she took her seat in her private chair on the platform.

In a very few words I introduced her as the Pastor Emeritus of the church and as the author of the textbook which I held in my hand. She then delivered her address.

During this address several healings took place; one in particular, an account of which was published in the Journal a few months afterwards. A man came in with two crutches, listened to her and went out without them. When he reached the house he was visiting on Tremont Street, his friends asked him where his crutches were; he said he did not know, he had never seen them since he went into that church and heard that woman talk. The janitor looked for the crutches but never found them.

Mrs. Eddy never spoke in public without healings taking place. The truth that she expounded would heal the sick and redeem the sinner, and it has gone around the world in its mission.

She told me afterwards that she liked my introduction.

Mrs. Eddy made a practice of doing things quickly when it was revealed to her that they should be done. In response to a demonstration, we saw the owner of 95 Falmouth Street for the first time on Christmas Eve. Christmas morning before eleven o'clock we had a contract for the house and had paid part of the purchase money as per agreement. We knew before we had finished the original Mother Church, judging from the constant growth of our audiences, that we should need a larger building and we should need all the property on that block for the purpose. Later on we purchased 97 Falmouth Street, all done in one day. 99 Falmouth Street hung along a while until Mrs. Bates received a telegram from Mrs. Eddy: "Buy Ninety-nine at once or you will never get it." The party who was to furnish the money for the purchase lived in a distant city, but Mrs. Bates, in response to this order, went to the real estate agent and bought the house that day. Next we bought Number 101 in a similar manner.

We were living in 97 Falmouth Street and had a year's lease of the house but were impressed to buy 103, which was on the corner of St. Paul Street. We had heard that it might possibly be purchased and the party lived near by. We called at their house and found that their goods were all packed preparatory to moving into 103 and occupying it for their home. They were in New York for a few days previous to making the change. We obtained the key from the person in charge, looked over the house and thought it best to act immediately. Mrs. Bates and I went to New York that night, taking a couple of sheets of legal cap paper with us, and at quite an unseemly hour the next morning, went uptown where the owners were living and found them at their breakfast table. We introduced the subject by saying that we had heard that they would sell 103 Falmouth Street.

The lady said, "No, we did offer it for sale, but we put it in good order and have our goods packed ready to move in when we return to Boston, which will be in a few days."

We had considerable conversation about it and the lady said she would go up to her husband's room (he always breakfasted in his room) and consult him.

He came downstairs in a few minutes and said, "Mr. Bates, I am going to sell you that house, and I will tell you why,—I know who you are, though I have never seen you before. You are helping Mrs. Eddy do her work, and I know all about you. My son was very sick last year and I told God if he was healed that the first chance I had to do anything for the Christian Scientists I would do it, and this is my opportunity. I do not want to sell the house but you can have it, and I think it is right. I am only keeping my vow with God to let you have the house."

I immediately drew up a contract, paid part of the purchase money on the house, and took the eleven o'clock train back to Boston, arriving there about five in the evening. The next morning

I had carpenters in the house making some changes which were necessary to our comfort. Later I received a telegram from the husband saying he would be in Boston that afternoon. He came to me and said, "Mr. Bates, this matter was closed too quickly. You are in possession of the house and all we have is a scrap of paper and a check."

I said, "The deed is still in your name. In addition to the deed, which is all you had before, you have my contract to purchase the house and you have my check for part payment, so you have a great deal more than you previously had."

"I did not think of that," he said.

"Yes," I added, "you are better off than you were before, and if you bring me a deed in ten days the money will be ready for the entire payment," and he said, "I don't know but you are right," and went off to New York perfectly happy.

Mrs. Eddy had many times told us, "If you have anything to do, do it quickly before the error gets hold of it and stops you," and we always tried to work on that plan. I recall one time she asked me why I put a certain lady on an important committee. I said, "Because she is a good healer and a good Scientist."

She said, "I have no use for her. I once told her to do something which was very important which should have been done at once. She was a whole year doing it. That is not the way to demonstrate Christian Science."

Miscellaneous Writings

In the fall of 1896, Mrs. Eddy called me to Concord and told me to buy the house known as 97 Falmouth Street and connect it to Number 95, which we were using as a Publishing House. She said, "Get your building arranged for business, buy a linotype and be prepared to work for me, as I am about to issue a new book."

We had just moved out of Number 97 to 103. We proceeded to make the purchase from one of our members who held the property and put the building in order for the work which was to be done there. We secured the linotype and installed it, and many other devices as accessories to printing work.

After a few weeks the copy came to be set up. A competent foreman printer was engaged who proved to be a very valuable man and served us many years. He had done the best class of work, was well educated, a good literary student, and an excellent proof reader. Others were employed, as well as an operator to work the linotype.

It was necessary for me to go to Syracuse about this time, and on my return I was accosted by persons in the Publishing House who asked me to help them on *Miscellaneous Writings*. "Why," I asked, "haven't you set up that book?" They said no, not a single sheet had been approved by Mrs. Eddy. I asked what they had been doing. They said they had been working hard but it was new work to them and time seemed to slip away without accomplishing anything. I took hold of the matter and in a couple of days got them organized and commenced to turn out some work.

Soon after this, Mrs. Eddy called me and told me that the work was not coming fast enough. She also said, "The people are ready for my book and it must come out. Do all you can to advance it."

Then the work began in earnest. The linotype was run constantly. Impressions were taken from the plates. They were read, corrected and the proof taken to Mr. John Wilson of Cambridge, a son of the original John Wilson who established in that city a printing house which had always published Science and Health. The proof sheets would usually be ready from eleven to one o'clock at night, and it was a part of my duty to take them to Mr. Wilson and have him read them over and make corrections. At that time the street car service in Boston was not good late at night, so it was necessary to hire a cab and retain it until Mr. Wilson had gone over the sheets. I then returned to the Publishing House where we made corrections and a messenger was called, who left about five in the morning to take an early train for Concord and submit the sheets to Mrs. Eddy. This was our daily work for several weeks.

I recall that after reading a larger part of the proof, Mr. Wilson said, "This will be a valuable book, and Mrs. Eddy will have a great sale of it."

I found that in order to accomplish what was necessary, I would be obliged to stay in the Publishing House until about six o'clock in the morning. I then went home, usually slept two hours, had a little breakfast and returned to the Publishing House.

During this busy time our two maids were taken seriously ill and it looked as though they might leave us together. Mrs. Bates had to give all her time to the care of them, and brought them through about the time that *Miscellaneous Writings* was completed. I would go into the house for a meal and sometimes get it, and other times find nothing to eat. Mrs. Bates was up night and day with the girls and there was no chance to cook anything and I had no time to go to a restaurant, so I took what I could get, and sometimes went without, satisfying myself with continuous work.

The result was that *Miscellaneous Writings* was brought out to Mrs. Eddy's satisfaction. When they were finally published, Mrs. Eddy sent me a beautiful watch chain, designed by herself, consisting of seven links, the gold of which was taken from her son's mine in Dakota. The design of the chain was a flat web of gold with a slab of quartz on either side; the gold turned over the edge, holding the slab secure. These slabs were full of beautiful stones and gold ore. Mrs. Eddy was told that her son's mine was the only one that produced them. It is an elegant piece of workmanship,—the most beautiful watch chain I ever saw. I prized it then and do now very highly. In her letter, Mrs. Eddy said she wished me to accept it as a favor from her for my work in helping her to get out the new book.

Miscellaneous Writings had a wonderful sale. It was advertised in the Journal, and over twenty-five thousand copies were subscribed and paid for before they were issued from the press. When they came in, we were very busy making up the distribution. The book was received with much approbation.

The year before I had asked Mrs. Eddy's permission to reprint some of the early numbers of the *Christian Science Journal* which contained articles from her pen. The number printed was small as there were but a few Scientists at the time, and it was very difficult to get the early numbers. I had succeeded in getting all of them myself, and as they contained valuable articles from Mrs. Eddy, I thought it would be a kindness to the new students to put them in their hands. Mrs. Eddy said, "Wait—I am getting out a book which will include all those articles of mine, as well as some of my addresses and sermons, and that will take their place." Further, she told me that when she wrote these articles she was extremely busy teaching classes, preaching on Sundays, and doing a vast amount of other work which occupied her time. Thus, the articles were written in a hurry and did not receive the care they should; also that she was now re-editing them and would bring them out in much better form than the originals. "Again," she said, "you must remember that the Journal had a good many contributions from students who were immature, and the writings are not strictly Scientific and I do not care to reproduce them."

I well remember how rejoiced we all were when we possessed a copy of *Miscellaneous Writings*.

I felt so deeply the value of *Miscellaneous Writings* that I was constrained to write to Mrs. Eddy the following letter:

"Boston, February 11, 1897.

"Rev. Mary Baker Eddy.

"Dear Mother:—To me, and I believe to the world, February tenth, 1897, is a Red Letter day in Christian Science. On this day, the first edition of *Miscellaneous Writings* was delivered at our Publishing House in Boston, and through the Publisher, Mr. Armstrong, distributed to all parts of our country, and to some foreign points. I believe I realize the truth of the following passage in Science and Health with Key to the Scriptures, to-day as never before,—'Divine Love always has met, and always will meet every human need.'

"On this day (February tenth) we enlarged our borders at the Publishing House. The need for larger quarters had been apparent for some time, and arrangements had been made to give more and better room to many of our departments. It may at first sight seem to be a singular coincidence that all this change, increase of space, and rearranging of our office work, should be accomplished on the very day that this new book was delivered to us, but such is the fact, and our efficient helpers are now in larger and more commodious rooms, which are adapted to the increased business of the Society. I am assured that in Science there are no happenings, but that all takes place according to the Divine order.

"Two years ago you gave us the Impersonal Pastor for our Mother Church, and soon afterward the same Pastor was appointed for all the branch churches. Now you give us the Impersonal Teacher. I wish I might find words adequate to express all that I feel in receiving this last great gift from you. I consider it the most valuable Book, aside from the Bible, ever published, with one exception only: i.e., Science and Health with Key to the Scriptures.

"I also believe that *Miscellaneous Writings* will be a great factor in the sale and distribution of our Text-Book, thereby proving itself a great blessing, not only for to-day, but for ages to come.

"There are several points about, and connected with, this Book which to me are significant. I noticed there are twelve chapters,—one for every tribe (or phase of belief).

"The third chapter contains sixty-four pages of Questions and Answers. If this chapter does not destroy the belief in the trinity of error, then printed matter can never accomplish that end. I further observe that this Book contains a large portion of your writings for fourteen years. This number is significant when I recall what has transpired during those years; also a remarkable prophecy, and its fulfillment, in just fourteen years, and its meaning in Christian Science. I am reading this Book carefully, and while I recognize many old friends which were in the Journal, yet there is much that is new to me.

"I am so much rejoiced to have, assembled with other articles, your letters to the Church, those to the First Members, and your sermons in the early days, as well as all the other warnings, admonitions and wise counsellings. I had never dared to hope for all this in one book which I could take in my hands and call my own. God is better to us than we ask or think.

"After reading *Miscellaneous Writings* one is impressed with the great fact that God has done this by the hand of His anointed. One more delightful experience in reading this Book is, that it takes us back to the classes in the Massachusetts Metaphysical College, and it seems as though we were sitting at your feet and being taught directly by you. Then again, what a blessing to those who were unable to enter your College, but have waited long years to do so! To them you speak, as of old you spoke to your students who were present, and these brothers and sisters who have been waiting and longing for this day are now fed, not with crumbs, but with meat from the table of our God, who is Life, Truth, and Love.

"Your affectionate student,

"Edward P. Bates."

The Fake Libel Suit

Mrs. Eddy frequently sent an address to The Mother Church to be read in the auditorium on Sunday. These addresses were exceedingly helpful to the members and covered a variety of subjects. Among others to be read, she sent an address which had copious quotations from the Book of Revelation, referring to the Babylonish

Woman. This was read and a short time thereafter a person said that Mrs. Eddy had libeled her, and she instituted a suit against Mrs. Eddy for an enormous sum of money. The suit was thoroughly tried out in the Boston papers, most of the articles published being from the pen of the plaintiff. This procedure continued until the courts took up the matter and served an injunction on the plaintiff, fining her for trying her case in the newspapers. Months elapsed during this procedure and there was much controversy over the case. Some of the students even admitted that Mrs. Eddy must have meant the plaintiff when she quoted the Scripture. They forgot the fact that Mrs. Eddy never personalized error,—she generalized it,— and in her various writings she states that error is the ape of Deity, which is universal good, and error would not be error unless it made the claim to be universal.

Early in January of the year in which the case was to be tried, Mrs. Eddy invited me to Concord to talk it over. Soon after I arrived there she said, "Mr. Bates, what do you think of my case?"

I told her that I was satisfied she would come off victorious in the suit. Further, I stated that on the previous Christmas Day, I was reading in the Bible the fifty-fourth chapter of Isaiah, and the fourth chapter of Micah, and it came to me like a revelation that these chapters foretold the result of the suit against Mrs. Eddy. She called

Dr. Frye to her side and asked him to take note of those chapters as she wished to read them carefully. I further said, "Mrs. Eddy, you will have 'to go down to Babylon and there you will be delivered.' The courts of the country are a Babel and you will have to go there, but you will have an easy victory!"

She said, "Do you believe it?"

I answered, "I am sure of it," and she dropped the subject. She wished to know where my thoughts rested and was satisfied.

During that visit, or soon afterwards, she asked me to name a competent attorney in Boston. She said attorneys had been recommended to her, but she did not think they were competent to carry her case and she wanted to know if I could name one who was. I told her I could not; that I had very little acquaintance with the lawyers in Boston, but if she wished I would find out and report to her. She gave me the commission. I quietly made inquiries, the result of which was that I was satisfied that the Honorable Samuel J. Elder was a superior lawyer, universally conceded to be the Dean of the Massachusetts Bar, and he was the man to carry her case intelligently.

I wrote her to this effect and she engaged Mr. Elder as her counsel. She then tried several of her students to act as intermediaries between her and the counsel, but did not seem to get the right person until she sent for Edward A. Kimball of Chicago. Mr. Kimball was a man of a logical and a legal mind and was well conversant with Science, having practised it for several years, and doing splendid work in that line. Mr. Kimball would go to Concord and stay perhaps one or two days and receive instruction from Mrs. Eddy. He would then come to Boston and spend one, two or three days in the office of Mr. Elder, closeted with him and talking over the case. Then he would return to Concord, get further instruction and again return to Mr. Elder. This continued for several months until the case went to trial, when the correctness of Mrs. Eddy's method of preparation became apparent.

When the court opened and the case was put on, the plaintiff's attorney read the complaint to the court, which complaint endeavored to show that Mrs. Eddy in quoting from Revelation meant the plaintiff. For two or three days witnesses were examined by the plaintiff's attorney and no evidence was produced to substantiate the claim. Some of the consulting attorneys wished to cross-examine the witnesses. Mr. Elder said, "No, they haven't proven anything, and if we should cross-examine them it might bring confusion into the case." Consequently, not a single witness was cross-examined.

The case continued until all the plaintiff's

witnesses were examined, then the plaintiff's counsel advised Mr. Elder that he rested his case. Mr. Elder arose from his chair in a most dignified, quiet, unassuming manner and addressed the Court substantially as follows: "May it please your Honor, the plaintiff has failed to make a prima facie case and I move that the Court instruct the jurors to bring in a verdict of no cause for action."

The Judge immediately arose and addressed the jury. "Gentlemen of the Jury: You will please retire to the anteroom and bring in a verdict of no cause for action," which was done.

Thus the case was thrown out of court without calling a single witness for the defendant, Mrs. Eddy.

The plaintiff's case had been tried in the newspapers. Mrs. Eddy's case was tried out by her in Concord; her instructions were given to Mr. Kimball, which he communicated to Mr. Elder; so that when we came into court, there was nothing to do but stay there and hear a supposititious case and then move for a non-suit.

Thus ended the fake libel suit.

The Concord Church

The services continued for several months in

Christian Science Hall with a rapidly increasing audience, until the room was not large enough to comfortably seat all who wished to attend. At this juncture, Mrs. Eddy decided to build a church on the lot where the Hall was located. She nominated three gentlemen of Concord as Trustees and conveyed the land to them to hold for the benefit of the church. She also gave them one hundred thousand dollars to build the church.

They immediately proceeded with its construction and would have made rapid progress with it but for the interference of a student, who, disobeying Mrs. Eddy's expressed wish, undertook to supervise the building operation and the details of finish.

In about a year the church edifice was erected and dedicated. In order to prepare for the dedication it was necessary to put in temporary windows. The window question had been argued between this student, the architect, the agent in New York, and the manufacturers who took the contract in Birmingham, England. There was plenty of money for the windows, which had been contributed by a branch church. If the matter had been left entirely to the Birmingham people, the church would have had windows, beautiful in color and design and artistic in effect; but every move they made was hindered by people who had no concept of the art; consequently, as stated above, the church was dedicated without the windows.

This state of affairs continued to exist for nearly a year after the dedication. Mrs. Eddy decided it was time to act. She called one of the building committee to her and said, "I wish you would have Mr. Bates go to Birmingham and get the windows." I was very much surprised one Monday while in Syracuse to receive a telegram from this gentleman requesting me to meet him the following day in Boston; I replied, naming the hour of ten and my house on Beacon Street as a place of meeting. He was there promptly and at once told me the nature of his errand, and asked me if I would go to Birmingham. I told him I would. He said, "When will you go?" I replied that I would sail the next Saturday if I could get a room on a steamer; I must return to Syracuse and make necessary arrangements as I should be absent a month or more and I should need two or three days to make my preparations. "I will leave it with you," he said. "Go and report what you do."

I immediately went to State Street where the steamer offices are located, called on all the agents of the European lines, and found only one room vacant for the following Saturday; all other accommodations were sold. I engaged this room, made a payment on it, and returned to Syracuse; completed my arrangements and proceeded to England.

I had fortified myself with letters from the building committee, the architect and the New York agent.

Arriving at Birmingham nine days later, I found that the Company, wearied of continued correspondence and criticism, changing of plans, and all that went with it, had begun to make the windows about the time I sailed from New York. I had a long interview with the president of the Company, whom I found to be a very agreeable gentleman.

In the afternoon the designing artist came in and we went through the window business very carefully. I was very much pleased with his conception of art glass, and learned that he had traveled to every principal city in Europe where there was a large cathedral or any building containing windows that were noted for their beauty or design; his education in this line seemed to be complete. In addition to this, he was very much of a gentleman in his manner, and we enjoyed the time spent with him exceedingly. He took me into the works and showed me the glass in the rough, the glass cut to make the figures, their manner of placing them, and then the way in which they tested the effect by placing them under a skylight and looking at the reflection in a large mirror placed on a table underneath the window, which gave them the effect they would produce when placed in position in a building.

I did not go to change the color or design in any way. I went for the windows and told them so. I left the color and design to the manufacturers.

They immediately put most of their workmen on our windows, and within a week I was able to report that one set of windows would be shipped in a Boston steamer the following Saturday, and the other would be shipped a week later. After satisfying myself that this would be done, I returned to New York and had the satisfaction of knowing that in a very short time the windows were placed in position and were acceptable to the building committee, Mrs. Eddy and the audience.

Mrs. Eddy had stated that she would not enter the church until it was complete and the windows in position. Soon after they were placed, Mrs. Eddy entered the church and expressed herself very well satisfied with the building and all its effects and decorations.

The Christian Science Board of Directors

Lest any person reading this brief history think that the Board of Directors were negligent in their duty in regard to building The Mother Church, I desire to put them right. I was thankful that the Board of Directors lived to attend the dedication of the church. Students less qualified in Christian Science might not have withstood the attacks which were directed against these gentlemen. It must be remembered that none of the Directors had much experience in building or in handling large bodies of men, and the matter of building The Mother Church was entirely out of their line. They, probably, with Mrs. Eddy's demonstration, could have carried on the work if they had been allowed to do so by the malpractitioners. Everything they undertook to do was thwarted, if possible. Constantly they had to work for themselves in Christian Science in order to exist. I know what I am writing as several persons who worked against them came into the First Member's meeting after the church was dedicated and told how they were instructed to work against the Board of Directors; a large group of students who followed a certain leader were gathered and instructed when to work and how to work, so that there was a continuous onslaught against the Directors. It was said that Mrs. Eddy did not wish the church to be built and had told the leader so, and she was carrying out Mrs. Eddy's wishes, while the Directors were disobeying them.

When I saw the condition of the church during the months of October and November, I knew that I could be of assistance to the Directors, but I had no inclination to give up my business and come to Boston for that purpose. It took a great deal of reasoning on my part to persuade myself that I was willing to do it, which, as I have said before, I finally did. I have worked many men in different lines, including construction of buildings, machinery, power plants, et cetera, since I was a very young man, and had the faculty of managing them and getting their good will. I came to Boston an unknown quantity to the malpractitioners. I slipped into the church almost unobserved and, while I had seven weeks of very difficult work, I suffered very little physically and was enabled to do the work which the Directors wished to do; consequently, I was freed from observations and attacks which, if it had been known I was there, might have laid upon me a heavy load.

The edifice was built as Mrs. Eddy directed, and completed when she directed it. Error did not delay the operation of building. Mrs. Eddy demonstrated and those who worked with her followed her demonstration and carried it to a success. It seemed at times that error would not only delay, but defeat the building operations, but it never did. We only needed to hold to the truth without reservation and the work was done. Mechanics working in the church said to me, at different times, "Mr. Bates, we start on a piece of work which we think will take us days or weeks, and before we know it the work is finished. What shall we do next?" And so through those seven weeks, work was performed which experts claimed it would take seven months to complete.

I was thankful that I saw the demonstration and

had the opportunity to learn what I did. Many times I was wavering in my faith, then I would hold to the thought of what was right in the case, what Mrs. Eddy was demonstrating, and what should be and what could be done, and it was done.

Thus you will perceive, if you imbibe this whole story, that the Directors did all they could under the conditions, and they came out of what might have been a disaster in good health and spirits. I was very glad I could be of service to those good men, and deserve no more credit than any other person who could do the same work.

What Mrs. Eddy Teaches

All through this article I have constantly spoken of Mrs. Eddy's teachings and demonstrations. I will now speak of them more specifically. Studying with her in three classes, and having many interviews with her in which she always talked about Christian Science and the way to demonstrate it, I feel that I know what she taught.

She divested us of the old theological idea of God as a limited Person, and gave us the better understanding of God as infinite, unlimited Good.

She taught us that man was the image and likeness of God, and that life is eternal.

She taught us to love our brother and how to love him, and what love is.

She imbued us with a love for spreading around the world the Gospel which had been revealed to her.

She taught many other things in her classes, and the teaching is still going on today and students can acquire it by a careful perusal of Science and Health with Key to the Scriptures, *Miscellaneous Writings, Unity of Good, No and Yes*, and her many other writings, together with her published addresses and sermons which have appeared from time to time in our periodicals. Every one of these has its value.

Was Mrs. Eddy Inspired?

She said she was.

Who could know better than she?

If she was inspired and knew it and did not say so, she would not be telling the truth.

How did she know that she was inspired?

Because when her ear was attuned to Good, she could hear the voice of God giving her the revelation of Christian Science and telling her how to record it.

She told me many times that God told her to write the book, Science and Health, but she said, "I simply held the pen." Frequently in conversation she would say, "Science and Health is God's word, and I have studied it all these years to learn what God said. What Mary thinks makes no difference; I want to know what God said."

Whoever heard of an author studying his book forty-four years to learn what he wrote? I believe there is no case parallel to this; Mrs. Eddy was a constant student of the book each and every day, and she frequently said she got new light on many subjects which she hoped sometime to be able to communicate to her students.

From the time I first met Mrs. Eddy, I never doubted that she was inspired of God to write Science and Health, and equally inspired to teach students and promulgate her works.

Do the Books of Prophecy Refer to Mrs. Eddy and Christian Science?

During two years while living in Boston, I spent most of my time studying the Book of Daniel, and what various authors said about it, especially regarding "Daniel's Dates." The Book of Daniel is a small one containing only twelve chapters, but it is a very important book to the Christian Scientist, and if you will read it with all the light that can be obtained upon it,—studiously, consistently and thoughtfully, I believe that you will come to the conclusion which was forced upon me, and that is that Daniel saw and defined that day when the Impersonal Christ should come to the world. It did come on the day which the most learned men in America and England claim, according to his prophecy, would be the second coming of Christ as Impersonal.

Dr. Seiss wrote a very interesting book over thirty years ago about the great Pyramid, entitled *A Miracle in Stone*. He spent eight years in Cairo studying the pyramid, and consulted with many students who had spent years of time and research on the pyramid, and he tells us that the passageway leading from the exterior of the Pyramid to the king's chamber has very significant marks upon the ramp stones in the passage; that the measurements carefully worked out indicate the exodus of the Hebrew Children from Egypt, the birth and ministry of Christ, and the advent of the Impersonal Christ in 1874, or about that time. [Mrs. Eddy refers to the Great Pyramid as "a miracle in stone" in Christian Healing, p.11, line 12.]

The revelation of Christian Science came to Mrs. Eddy in 1866, and she published her textbook, Science and Health, in 1875. These dates are significant. Ancient prophecy coincides with modern revelation. It all occurs according to the

Divine Order.

Mrs. Eddy worked her lifetime to spread through the world her doctrine of goodwill to man, scientific healing and regeneration, which comes through a clear apprehension of the Divine Mind and man made in His image and likeness, having dominion over everything unlike God. She worked to establish her church on a firm foundation in order that it should carry forward this work, either with or without her personality. Her leaving this plane caused no cessation of this work, but it continues in ever-multiplying ratio, establishing justice and righteousness. Mrs. Eddy gave us the only written rule by the use of which, hypnotism is dethroned, and Truth is revealed as supreme.

What more shall we say of this good woman? She was the best, purest, noblest and grandest woman that ever lived. She was so full of good works that to know her was to admire and love her. It would be easy to write volumes, and yet the completeness of her work would not be told. Let us quote the third verse from the twelfth chapter of Daniel:

"And they that be wise shall shine as the
brightness of the firmament; and they
that turn many to righteousness as
the stars for ever and ever."

13725766R00056

Made in the USA
Charleston, SC
28 July 2012